Architecture and Beyond

Edited by Christopher Procter and Fernando Rihl

with contributions by Anya Gallaccio, Carlos Eduardo Dias Comas, Nigel Coates, and Marcus Field

Artifice
books on architecture

Acknowledgements

For this, our first book, we have invited contributions from people who; have taught us, collaborated with us, written about us, hired us, or mentored us. We hope these voices will help readers to understand the different aspects of our work.

Christopher Procter and Fernando Rihl

We also would like to thank those who supported this project:

Anya Gallaccio, Carlos Eduardo Dias Comas, Nigel Coates, Marcus Field, Kelly Eginton, Gaetano Santaniello, Claudio Mattos Fonseca, Cynthia Caprara, Harry Willis-Fleming, Tomris Tangaz, Neusa Oliveira, Rogerio Prates, Sue Barr, Nelson Kon, Leonardo Finotti, Marcelo Nunes, Cyril Shing, Susannah Hagan and Vicky Richardson.

Contents

Anya Gallaccio
Introduction
<u>Fusing Modernity with the Picturesque</u>

Anya Gallaccio is a British installation artist. She was born in Paisley and studied at Kingston Polytechnic (1984–1985), and Goldsmiths College, London (1985–1988). Gallaccio creates site-specific installations, often using organic materials as her medium. She was shortlisted for the Turner Prize in 2003, and has exhibited extensively on an international level with work featured in numerous public and private collections worldwide. She lives and works in San Diego and London.

My experiences with Procter-Rihl studio have often been collaborative. While we've worked together formally on projects, more to the point, we maintain a relationship as peers, consulting with one another often. Their own collaboration sustains a balancing act of distinct personalities. Fernando is quick, surveying the scene for its limits, making spot-on assessments and bold suggestions. Chris jumps to action weighing out the possibilities. He gently steers the conversation toward resolution, assessing what's possible, how far boundaries can be pushed. Their partnership delivers an architecture with a fine resolution but also important work that is innovative and original.

Architecture interests me as a site-specific discipline. Procter-Rihl's relationship to context is not purely climatic but also, cultural and historical. Their architectural projects play with local symbols and archetypes fused with digital techniques in the investigation of space. This design strategy is an interesting way to work with the familiar, which becomes a communication tool between the object and its users. Their designs distill to something essential but not neutral; unafraid to impose unexpected materials and colours, play with unexpected movement, or imply subtle innuendo, their approach is inventive, courageous, and playful. By playing on forced perspectives and spatial illusions they provide a rich and stimulating experience of space. Their work is active, generating spaces to be occupied, objects to be handled and used, to be made your own. Forms are not gratuitous but a balance between the functional and the experiential blurring the boundaries of the pragmatic and the poetic.

The studio is interested in craft as a cultural expression of a place and time. Craft here is defined as the anthropological relationship between the body, material, concept and object in the production of domestic artefacts. Procter-Rihl sees making as an intrinsic part of the design process leaving no distinction between theory and practice. This research approach inevitably generates innovation as theory and practice continuously feed into each other. Local materials and traditional methods are subverted by pushing the boundaries of contemporary digital processes of making.

Landscaping has no subordinated role here but is as important as the architecture they create fusing sensitivity for British picturesque with an appreciation of Brazilian modernist landscapes. Their preference for native plants comes from a well-rounded conceptual approach, where aesthetics and ethics work in tandem to form their vision. In their landscape design, there is always a wild card, an unexpected and unpredictable dialogue in the continuous evolution between house and garden, a give and take between the presumptive hierarchy of shelter.

I hope readers will enjoy being led through Procter-Rihl studio's practice by this unusually structured presentation. The book is not compiled in a chronological order or by typology but instead reveals their design process and sketches outlines of thought through its four chapters. Readers are invited to draw connections and associations between the 42 richly illustrated projects within, following their evolution of thought and reinvention.

Humour and wit explored through unusual scenarios. Slice House pool, p 46.

The Pedestrian Roundabout Garden, p 70. Wyvil Meadow Garden Vauxhall, London 2015, where artificial meets natural.

Tableau Garden, Chelsea Flower Show 2000, p 80. Terrace grid to host an ornamental vegetable and flower garden.

Nigel Coates
Taxonomy in Practice

Between the Universal and the Eccentric

Roberto Burle Marx, (garden) Oscar Neimeyer Tremaine House, Santa Barbara, CA, USA, 1948. Image from model.

Levittown USA, production house with FL Wright influences, Rancher model No 4, Alfred Levitt, 1950. Bernard Hoffman/ TimeLife Pictures Getty Images.

Sibley/Pyramid House, Warren, Vermont, USA built 1967 architects William Reineke and David Sellers, image by Trillium1000 (Own work) [CC BY-SA 4.0 (http://creativecommons.org/licenses/by-sa/4.0)], via Wikimedia Commons.

Nigel Coates is often described as one of Britain's most original thinkers. His work engages with a wide variety of disciplines including architecture, design, art direction and latterly, art practice. After training at the Architectural Association, Coates' subversive spirit first came to public attention in 1984 with the formation of the NATO group (Narrative Architecture Today). Having led Architecture at the Royal College of Art in London from 1995–2011, he is now RCA Professor Emeritus.

Nigel Coates: I know Fernando and Chris from when they taught under me in the architectural programme at the Royal College of Art in London. They, like myself, have worked across the disciplines of architecture and design throughout their practice. Here, I have asked them a series of questions to understand what drives their work and structures this publication.

NC: What are your design aspirations for your professional collaboration?

Chris Procter: We wanted to develop a cross-disciplinary practice as we see the definition of architecure more fluidly than many other architecural practices. Our AA education has led us to this ethos of transgression and cross-fertilisation, elements we pursue in our studio. It is not a question of opportunities but of choice. We enjoy and intend to continue this, as one discipline feeds into another.

NC: The city offers a wide spectrum of different cultures, especially London where over 250 languages and cultures cohabit together. How do your origins in Brazil and the US come through in your work? And how does being based in London impact your work?

Fernando Rihl: Our inspirations are a fusion of our background and new influences around us. Design, for us, is a personal investigation, a reflection of our memories and previous experiences and how we perceive the world today. My Brazilian background, and so too Chris' background, will inevitably come through our work and current influences around us. London has a vast art and design community. It creates a great momentum where it is not only about being creative but also being original.

CP: Fernando and I are both of the new world, of Southern bold expression and Northern technical optimism. I grew up on the USA's East Coast in a new town, Levittown, the first American suburb, built in the 1950s along the lines of a Ford assembly line. 17,000 houses with one house finished every 16 minutes in full swing. Alfred Levitt, a Frank Lloyd Wright apprentice, had a strong interest in technology. His designs include features ahead of their time: open plan, radiant underfloor heat, thermopane windows, built-in kitchen countertop food processors, central air conditioning. Later, we moved to rural Vermont where we built several timber sustainable houses heated by wood. I was influenced by the ski holiday homes with soaring double-height spaces. Influences on me include American architects such as David Sellers from Yale and his self-built structures at Goddard College, as well as Paolo Soleri, John Lautner, and Charles Moore. So technology and expressive spaces were part of my personal history and now our current work.

NC: Your work follows a very specific method and impacted on how you structured this book. You could have done this by scale or place; how did you come up with these four sections?

CP: We could have followed a more traditional structure, chronologically, by scale or by location but we prefer to reveal our process as well as the final outcome. We limited the scope here to four actions as an introduction to some of our work. Readers will trace similarities employed across scales or disciplines.

FR: Our design method is based on linguistics through the investigation of spatial verbs. Some actions are regularly revised with different scales, programmes or contexts. It is a transformative process when you change discipline, scale or programme: conceptually, formally and technically. It is a fluid method of reinterpretation, sometimes an unconscious act, or sometimes, a result of analysis of other factors such as context, spatial experience or technology.

NC: Where do these operations sit within the design process? Are they targets or post rationalised?

FR: They are our firestarters to our formal investigations. They appear in our design process as a palette of options to be tested. They are active in our design process and become a way for us to synchronise our design moves with other concerns such as context, spatial experience, language, typology, etc. It is an evolutional process and not as clean or pure as it seem to be. There is the question of meaning and communication and often they are hybrid actions or doubled up actions.

NC: Folding has been a hobby horse for many architects; are you fans of Gilles Deleuze and Paul Virilio's ideas?

FR: Yes their ideas of oblique and seamless spaces did impact on our work to a certain extent but they have not dictated our design methods. Deleuze's concept of a continuous smooth seamless space is intriguing for our studio from the experiential point of view. We are interested in how the body moves along the space questioning the information that is identifying it. It is a question of experience and phenomenology.

CP: Deleuze's ideas led architects to explore extremely complex aesthetics. The "oblique" of Paul Virilio and Claude Parent removes the horizontal and vertical axis merging into one new inclined plane, radical but impractical in habitable spaces. The parametric design methods revisited the dissolution the of orthogonal in architecture as a new form of the "oblique", which can be disorienting and formally overworked. Limited diagonal folding of walls or roof planes within an orthogonal system can manipulate our perception of the space in more interesting ways. Perspectival foreshortening tells us about distance subliminally. The mind assumes balance and misreads the affects of the one plane out of the orthogonal assuming it is orthogonal space. Familarity with a glitch. This controlled use of diagonals throughout our work is explored as a contrasting plane to the orthogonal grid. Modernism employed glass walls to expand space. Perspectival manipulation is a more contemporary way to explore the illusion of spaces as it avoids thermal imbalances created by large areas of glass planes.

NC: There are many examples of encyclopedic organisation; Diderot's in the 2013 Venice Biennale had the theme of The Encyclopedic Palace. Is your modest version also intended to be all encompassing? Books can proffer taxonomies and as such, encompass universality; how does yours accommodate exceptions and eccentricities?

FR: The method should not be perceived as universal, by any means. It reflects how we explore some of our formal concerns. Other elements come into play such as context, orientation, programme, spatial experience meaning, signs, symbols, archetypes and typologies, not necessarily in this order. The exceptions occur when the programme requires more complexity leading to double-coding or hybrid actions. We do not see the method as restrictive. On the contrary, it gives us a structure to develop and test a wide range of ideas. I hope readers will find connections and similarities to engage with our design process. I hope readers will enjoy the way we structured the book revealing the process and how similar design actions get reinvented and reinterpreted in different projects and scales.

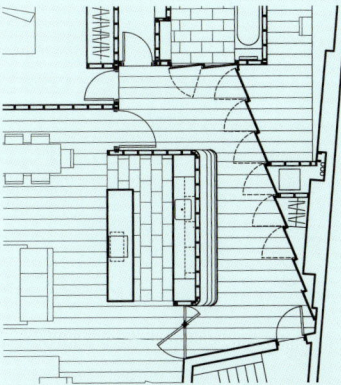

Canyon Apartment, p 38. The tilted wall creates a powerful vanishing point.

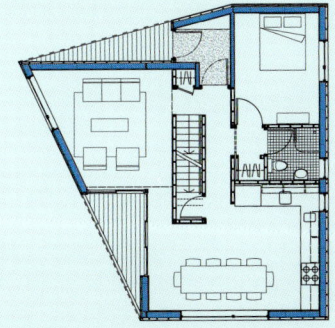

Pull House, p 20. Corner pulled away creating diagonals and covered exterior triangular porches.

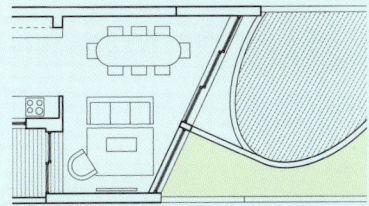

Three Ellipses Extension, p 66. Garden wall tilted towards the south maximises daylight and makes the extension appear wider.

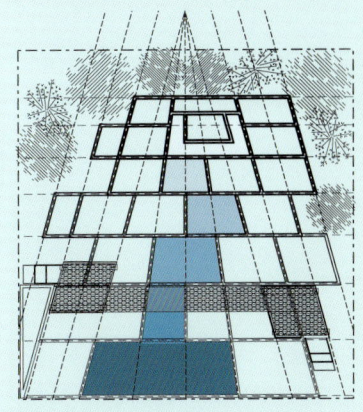

Chelsea Flower Show, p 80. Perspective diagonal grid emphasises depth.

Fernando Rihl
TransLocal
Beyond the Vernacular

The studio focuses on the reinterpretation of vernacular typologies.

Pull House, p 20, employs local materials with a new dying technique of double-colouring, 2004.

Brazilian typology for Nonoai project 2015. Reserva do Ibiopoca, MG, Brazil.

Affonso Reidy, MAM, Rio de Janeiro, 1952.

Alvaro Siza, IC Museum, Porto Alegre, Brazil, 2008.

Fernando Rihl is a co-founder of Procter-Rihl Architects, a multi-disciplinary practice developing design, landscape and architecture in the UK and abroad. Fernando studied in Brazil, where he completed his BArch at UFRGS and was awarded first prize in the Annual Brazilian National Student Competition among 55 national schools of architecture. At the Architectural Association (AA), Fernando pursued graduate studies in two fields, Housing Studies, 1991, and Environment and Energy, 1993, before completing his PhD, also at the AA, on daylight and phenomenology, 1998. He is currently a Lecturer at Royal College of Art, London, from 2006 to the present and Senior Lecturer at Chelsea College of Art, 2000 to the present.

In a hyper-modern world with greatly increased mobility and communication, how does architecture engage in the local versus the global debate? How to find a balance between the new and the everyday? Can architecture still relate to specific cultural patterns and local practices? Is there such a thing as an "architecture of cultural specificity"?

We are living in "post post times", with tensions from radical technological progresses and new ways of accessing, communicating and exchanging information with each other creating multiple cultural overlays in our everyday activities. Our current dilemma is similar to the position of a "trapeze", moving us through a continuous flux of information, managing the absurdities of our times full of incoherencies and ambiguities. Reality has become blurred with the virtual world. We not only embrace the virtual, but we accept it as real in our everyday activities. Baudrillard defines this moment as "death of the real where society's views of the world are radically affected by media and technology in a simulated environment".[1] Information has never travelled so fast and we have never been more connected to other cultures and behaviours than we are now. To a certain extent, we have all become global or universal. Some critics argue, therefore, that there is no place for a regional culturally specific approach to design, since the conditions of late capitalism and globalisation neutralise local identity and make us all part of a "global village". Others defend the contrary, that today's cultural overlays reinforce an even stronger need for identity and place. As Lyotard points out, "information travels radically faster nowadays than ever before generating a stronger need to differ and to declare one's identity and culture".[2] Human nature is far too diverse to fully relate to universal truths and argues for a multiplicity of theoretical standpoints rather than the grand gesture suggesting the replacement of what he calls metanarratives with local narratives or "petit recits". Procter-Rihl believes that architecture should respond to this binary condition. We have all become part of a global scenario but it is also part of human nature to identify and congregate in groups or subgroups with specific cultural patterns and practices. To deny this need to be unique is to oversimplify the human psyche.

The studio advocates for a new approach in architecture named TransLocal, where the familiar and the extraordinary, or the local and the global, blur together. Such issues have been tackled in the past by Critical Regionalism but TransLocal does not restrict itself to the Modernist aesthetic.[3] It seems incoherent to discuss identity and place and completely deny the importance of architectural archetypes and local symbols. The familiar is explored through local archetypes, signs, symbols, local materials and building technologies in response to place, climate, geography, cultural and historical contexts. The familiar goes beyond the vernacular and its associations of the domestic, the traditional and folklore. "Being local does not mean opposing modernisation, rationalisation or technological processes. It is not about romanticism nor theatricality, which can produce sameness and cultural regression."[4] For the studio, to be local is to respond to specific behavioural patterns and communities that engage place and culture at a particular time. The local can be a combination of current contextual identities not necessarily traditional in a true sense. For the studio, to be local means to embrace change and new cultural interventions. It is about the investigation of specific current behaviours of a given group but not cultural synthesis.

The extraordinary comes into play as an injection of the unexpected to local identity. It explores the imaginative, the spontaneous, the peculiar, and the original in architecture. Sameness is left aside. For the studio, one way the extraordinary is explored is through an architecture of the oblique with its forced perspectives and other spatial illusions. The "oblique' has been pursued in the past by Virilio and Parent (1963)and, more recently, by Parametric Design leading to a complete dissolution of planes.[5] But unlike parametric the studio pursues clarity and purity within an aesthetic of complexity where the orthogonal and the oblique play against each other. Familarity with a glitch. The body in motion plays a major role in this experience where users are challenged on their assumptions and expectations of size, geometry or materiality. Space becomes richer when the decoding process has a more complex nature but balanced where excitement does not become overpowering and autocratic. The aim is to create an architecture that challenges and engages users with unique spatial conditions. Materiality is played towards the digital sensibility with lightness and transience. These conditions are explored through structural delicacy, structural instability, and materials with ethereal qualities such as transparent and translucent elements within a synthetic colour palette. Assumptions of structural behaviour and stability are questioned in our architecture to create complexity and spatial ambiguity. The aim is to bring a sense of surprise into the equation countering sameness or neutrality.

TransLocal can be identified at different scales in our practice, from public realm projects to product design. The studio always aims to find a balance between the functional and the psychological, regardless of the scale of the intervention. Our designs are absolutely clear and confident about the purposes they serve. We aim to design objects that trigger our memories and imagination beyond the functional agenda. They are, in this sense, functional artefacts, but they are also part of a symbolic system. As Pallasmaa states, "… as we construct our self-made world, we construct projections and metaphors of our own mindscapes".[6]

Making is a key investigation tool in our design process. It is a key expression of the "local" where art and craft strategies are fused together. The studio aims to narrow the gap between practice and theory working on an interactive flow of "thinking through making and making through thinking".[7] Making is explored as a speculative, interactive and experimental practice without pre-determined scenarios. By a series of "regulated improvisations", we look to maximise the full potential or to push the limits of a specific tool or machinery. The process becomes an in-depth understanding of a technique looking for design opportunities to be explored. Tim Ingold defines this moment as "knowing from inside" where there is an in-depth knowledge of its methods with no preconceived ideas of how best to make things.[8] Sennett highlights this method as a seamless fusion with no distinction between the theorist and the craftsman. Innovation appears effortlessly as a result of expressing the limitations of a process, by employing a material that is not normally associated with a specific process or by swapping a material that contradicts its experience. Innovation is achieved as theory and practice continuously feed into each other where traditional methods are mixed with computational processes It is a celebration of craft but also aims to reinvent its processes bringing something new or unusual to the mix.

Design for us, regardless of its scale, is a practice that captures the insights of imagination but also immediately connects and engages with the material world. It is about creating a balance of exploring dreams and coaxing materials. It should connect to culture and place with familiar symbols or archetypes. The message has to be subliminal, otherwise, it is overpowering and short-lived. For the studio, the key is to suggest, creating a long-lasting experience: slightly unclear, hazy, and not easily readable surrounded by a range of references, associations, memories, and experiences. As the mind decodes spaces through our memories, it may lead to zones that are beyond the grasp of reason, making the experience a truly personal discovery.

Vilanova Artigas, Bus terminal JAU, Sao Paulo, Brazil 1973.

The studio makes no distinction between the theorist and the craftsman.

1. Baudrillard, Jean, *Simulacra and Simulation*, 1981.
2. Lyotard, Jean-François, "Answering the question: What is Postmodernism?", *The Post-Modern Reader collected essays*, ed Charles Jencks, John Wiley & Sons, 2011.
3. Canizaro, Vicenzo, *Architectural Regionalism, Collected Writings on Place, Identity, Modernity, and Tradition*, NY: Princeton Architectural Press, 2007.
4. Tonzis, Alexander and Liane Lefaivre, *Critical Regionalism, Architecture and Identity in a Globalized World*, London: Prestel, 2003.
5. Virilio, Paul and Claude Parent, *Architecture Principe 1966/1996*, trans George Collins, Paris: Les Éditions de L'Imprimeur, 1997.
6. Pallasmaa, Juhani, *The Thinking Hand, Existential and Embodied Wisdom in Architecture*, AD Primers, John Wiley & Sons, UK, 2009.
7. Sennett, Richard, *The Craftsman*, London: Penguin, 2008.
8. Ingold, Tim, *Making, Anthropology, Archaeology, Art and Architecture*, Routledge, 2013.

Christopher Procter
Peak Performance
Towards a new Eco Revolution

Earthship houses built with rammed earth, tires and recycled bottles, Taos, New Mexico, USA.

Earth-cast concrete domes, Arcosanti, Arizona USA 1974.

The influential tool catalog published by Stewart Brand, 1968–1980.

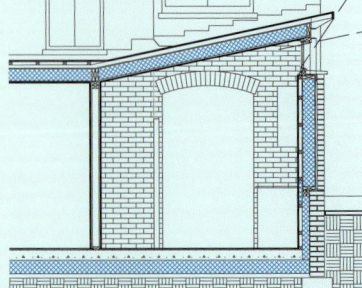

Prefab 200 mm (8") Structural Insulated Panels wrapping Scoop Extension, p 42, London 2013.

Christopher Procter a co-founder of Procter-Rihl Architects, a multi-disciplinary practice developing design and architecture in the UK and abroad. He studied in the USA at Carnegie Mellon and in London at the Architectural Association. He apprenticed with Paolo Soleri in Arizona. He has past experience in practice with Rick Mather, Allies + Morrison, Jestico + Whiles, in London, Peter Woerner in New Haven, and WYS Architects in NYC. Currently he is a lecturer in Architecture at the Royal College of Art where he teaches new building technologies.

Environmental strategies, today, have changed from the nascent 1970s roots of the movement. Traditionally, the 1970s eco-warrior distanced himself from society creating alternative communities in isolated places such as Lindesfarm Scotland, Earthship biotecture in Taos, New Mexico, or Paolo Soleri's Arcosanti in Arizona. This demographic followed a utopian agenda, removing themselves from a world of destruction and developing a new attitude towards nature. This disillusioned group employed innovative and forgotten vernacular building technologies within a communal or consensus social structure. These colonies aimed not only to revolutionise building but were experimenting with social structures.

Environmentalists, today, act from within society focusing on energy efficiency. They are the neighbour next door implementing developed low carbon technologies creating a quiet, but effective revolution. They have swapped the *Whole Earth Catalog* for the internet, the wood burner for the Tesla Powerwall home battery. They are part of a growing mainstream acceptance that earth is not a never-ending supplier of resources and that something needs to be done. This new environmentalist is more strategic than its predecessors. They acknowledge that to implement renewal technology in any transformative way, mitigating severe climate change, it has also to be purvasive and financially sustainable. Off-grid is highly desirable, but selling energy back to the common grid requires change to the distribution system itself. Some forward thinking governments in Europe and America agree, and see the benefits of infinate localised renewable energy producers over a few large fossil fuel power plants.

Procter-Rihl approaches sustainability by maximising energy performance using new building materials and technologies. Built-in energy harvesting can now power our electric lives. Solar photovoltaic electrical panels are now a mature technology with reliable components, efficient grid tied reverse metering, and performance monitoring panel by panel sent to your smart phone. LED lighting, electric induction cook tops, and the internet of things smart monitoring will maximise the use of energy generated. Careful construction detailing and real world understanding of heat flows is progressing exponentially. The German Passivhaus standards have resulted in a fuller understanding of the physics and pushed component research in insulation and glazing systems. Efficient industrialised production of Passivhaus certified windows is meeting this new demand for triple-glazed carefully sealed units well beyond modernist standards of double-glazing. Working as a facilitator, our projects follow our client's commitment and aspirations. Architecture can no longer be solely an aesthetic exercise but must address our new reality of a world on the brink of climate change. The studio aims to bring together sustainable issues with conceptual ideas to create an integrated and balanced architecture that serves its time, culture, and place.

Early twentieth-century Modernism brought us technology to dematerialise building skins predicated on carbon based energy. New research gives us the materials and understanding to make these skins intelligent in collecting solar energy and controlling thermal flows. This is a radical change as big as Modernism's break from traditional architecture. As architects today, we must grab this opportunity to create a new architecture operating at peak performance.

Carlos Eduardo Dias Comas
Double-Coded

Reflecting on the Post Post Times

Carlos Eduardo Comas studied architecture in Porto Alegre (Universidade Federal do Rio Grande do Sul), Philadelphia (University of Pennsylvania) and Paris (Université de Paris-Saint Denis) and has written and lectured extensively on Modern Brazilian Architecture and Urbanism both in his native country and abroad. He is full Professor at Universidade Federal do Rio Grande do Sul and editor of its Graduate Program in Architecture journal _ARQTEXTO_. His private work includes a series of residences, art galleries and the Porto Alegre Central Market working with architects Claudio Araujo and Carlos Fayet as well as structural engineer Eladio Dieste. Co-curator with Barry Bergdoll and Jorge Francisco Liernur of the exhibition Latin America in Construction: Architectures 1955–1980, March 2015 at MoMA, New York.

Preston Robinson House, Williamstown, MA, USA, 1947. Designed by Marcel Breuer, Archives of American Art, Smithsonian Institition. Photo by Robert Damora.

In his book, *The Shape of Time*, George Kubler states that "the moment of an artist's entrance is the moment in the artistic tradition with which his biological opportunity coincides. It is as important as his temperament or training, and conditions what he can and what he cannot do in terms of asserting his presence."[1] Procter-Rihl, a London based design studio founded in 1995 by two former AA students, came of age in the 2000s with two residential projects, Slice House, a town house in Porto Alegre, Brazil and Pull House, a rural residence in Brattleboro, Vermont, USA.

Pampulha Yacht Club, Oscar Niemeyer, MG, Brazil, 1942.

This was a post postmodernism and a post-deconstruction age. Once again a minimalist modern sensibility triumphed. Like many of their peers, Procter-Rihl embraced the reduction of the primary elements of architecture to their essential geometry where walls, floors and roofs should be conceived as plates if not planes. Nonetheless, they shunned the usual corollaries of that position in Britain or Iberia, distancing themselves from minimalist modern architects like John Pawson or Alberto Campo Baeza. They would rather reinterpret orthogonal space through planar manipulation. The modernist block has been the norm for far too long and it had become just plane boring.

Slice House, p 44, folded roof by Procter-Rihl, Porto Alegre, RS, Brazil, 2004.

Procter-Rihl do not dispute its practical convenience. However, the dislike remained, and posed a question. What do you do when you want to break out of the box without erasing it completely, as current digital architecture does? The modern tradition offered at least three options combinable between them. One could qualify the homogeneity of the box, suggesting its decomposition through the use of different materials, textures, patterns, colours, etc. One could also question the integrity of the box by subtraction or addition, either by cutting holes, chopping corners, setting up protrusions, developing extensions and creating layered deep facades. Finally, one could question its precise orthogonality by slanting, bending, twisting walls or roofs: operations identifiable as distortion and implying, at the same time, an attack on its integrity even if limited in scope, affecting only one of its constituent planes or plates.

Artigas' second residence by Vilanova Artigas, Sao Paulo, Brazil, 1949.

Le Corbusier was quick to point out some ways of breaking the box that satisfied the spirit. The polychromy of the walls went a long way to dissolve the massiveness of the cheap and blocky Pessac houses, otherwise enlivened by thin concrete vaults covering terraces over ground carports. Ribbon windows extended along the main facades of the white walled, blocky and luxurious Villa Stein at Garches dissolving its corners. Raising Villa Savoye on stilts amounted to slicing its ground floor, while the second floor terrace read as an excavation. The unbuilt but influential Errazuris house introduced the butterfly roof as an elementary distorting act.

Moreover, Brazilian and American examples of a broken box were conspicuous. Butterfly roofs distinguished vintage icons such as Niemeyer's Yacht Club at Pampulha and Breuer's Robinson House. Monopitch roofs enriched the silhouette of Niemeyer's Ouro Preto Grand Hotel and Lucio Costa's Nova Friburgo Park Hotel as well as Charles Moore's Sea Ranch. Angled walls suggested cut-outs in Johnson and Burgee's Pennzoil Place.

Artigas' house, as above. Tilted planes and roof break the traditional modernist cube.

Sobrados House in Porto Alegre, Brazil.

Slice House, p 44, Porto Alegre, Brazil.

Pull House, p 20, Brattleboro, VT, USA.

Accordian Terrace housing, p 30, London.

Cobogó low cost housing, p 101, Brazil.

Brazil low cost housing studies.

In this context Procter-Rihl take an eminently sensible step further. They choose to intensify distortion as a key design strategy. Distortion could have a rather pragmatic experiential justification, both Procter and Rihl spoke persuasively about this. But there is more to distortion in terms of meaning. It is resistance to the mediocre norm. It is affirmation of the traditional extra ordinariness of architecture within the built environment. Contemporary, it relied upon computing technology to bring and tie together precisely a bunch of skewed planes. Retrospective, it hinted at erudite modern references at the same time that it evoked venerable but geometrically supple vernacular workmanship. Last but not least, distorting the box from dice to diamonds was like having your cake and eating it too. The volumes that could result from it were both dissimilar in geometrical terms and identical from the viewpoint of topology.

At the same time, following the oldest modern tradition, Procter-Rihl wanted to keep light their spiced up broken box. They disliked Brutalist and neo-Brutalist heaviness, even if enlivened by holes and cut outs. Nonetheless, they knew all too well that architecture could not be built as an origami exercise, for walls and roof (or floors, for that matter) were not to be confounded, their reduction to planes being valid as mental operation but not as hard fact. The expression of weightlessness had to be achieved without sacrificing the requirements of pragmatics and tectonics. Contrary to minimalist pursuits, thickness or depth mattered in solid as well as layered, composite, hybrid walls, roofs or floors; so did surface, and variety of surface corresponding and expressing a diversity of architectural situations in the Information Age. In terms of heritage, it meant favoring the sensibility toward materials and mass and siting of the Carioca school of modern architecture rather than that of the Paulista one, siding with Venturi against Rudolph or Mies, and placing the Grays above the Whites.

The two first houses by Procter-Rihl demonstrate how their general compositional and constructive principles acquire particular character, in correspondence with their situations. Slice House comments on the accidental nature of the wedge-like corner plot, an impossibly narrow residue resulting from the extension of a street across a half built block. At the same time, it points to the revelatory nature of the house's key element, the long facade endowed with the opacity of a party wall. The geometry of its volume relates to the nineteenth-century sobrados of Porto Alegre. Besides visually disjoining the facets of the distorted box, its heterogeneous materiality calls to mind the local interest in Brutalist heavy lightness as much as the casualness and precariousness of self-built housing. Raw and rough, the reinforced concrete long facade shelters a fully glazed internal patio. The metallic roof and narrow entrance facade add sparkle, pattern, relief, and a note of flimsiness, although the spiced up broken box is also a well-crafted one. Pull House is about the way the timber panels rise and enclose the faceted volume of a latter day Vermont barn (or New England saltbox) as much as it is about the ambivalent reading of volumetric cut-outs as displacements, or surfaces fractured through the use of dark and light stains, the discontinuity of colour in the same plane creating an illusory fold, a virtual origami. Conversely, one wall is assimilated to the roof by using aluminum sheets as rain screen, the continuity of material suggesting another fold, less illusory than its painted counterpart and more contrived than the ridge it echoes.

The Accordion Terrace, 2013, is a spin-off of the Mansard House plans featuring a pleated front facade that evokes the bow windows of brick Victorian row houses. Distortion loses its picturesque accidental character and turns into a serial pattern, as befits the repetitive programme and a generic site. Procter-Rihl show once again that respecting the spirit of the place does not preclude inventiveness, blending in does not imply blandness. Distortion allows Procter-Rihl's interventions to blend in and stand out at the same time. Their suave yet strong character binds together the disparate components of the urban blocks into which they fit in Brazil and England. A set of competition schemes show patterned distortion applied to low-rise apartment buildings occupying whole urban blocks. The three-storied Cobogó low-cost housing proposal, 2010, responds to very tight budgetary constraints and a real site in Brazil's biggest port, Santos, near São Paulo. The housing strips sport small interior courtyards that recall some PROPAR-sponsored projects of the 1980s.[2] The regularly pleated rooves correspond to regularly pleated long facades, enlivened by the alternate disposition of openings and irregularly coloured blank panels in the different floors. The pleating comes out as a rationalisation of Gaudi's La Pedrera or some Roberto Brothers' projects of the 1950s, such as the Marques do Herval office building in Rio's downtown. The box is broken rhythmically. The Moscow perimeter block, 2010–2012, of the same height envisages ideal sites, and a higher income tenancy. Despite the flat roofs, liveliness increases as pleats alternate by floor combined with triangular balconies, freestanding columns frame the access to the large internal green space with underground parking and shops occupy the ground floor corners. The results are promising rather than conclusive. The materiality of the projects is not really defined apart from the indication of lightness. Nevertheless, their geometry confirms Procter-Rihl's consistency, and points to an eventually fruitful symbiosis with their furniture work such as the highly suggestive Super8 screen or Topo shelving systems.

The powerful association between Burle Marx and the Carioca school suggested that landscape architecture was another weapon that Procter-Rihl could wield to assert their presence in the contemporary scene, and they did not fail to recognise it, aligning themselves occasionally with the art-borrowed innovations that people like Martha Schwarz introduced in the late 1980s. Dream-like, ambivalent connotations that generic distortion may carry are very much in evidence in many projects. A skewed metallic grid makes up the theatrical backbone of the precious water garden designed for the Chelsea Flower Show, 2000. Extruded wedge cone structures pop out of the paved surfaces of Lunatic Garden, 2004. The squarish wild garden at the forecourt and a long mixed border done with native plantings both intensify and deny the rough urbanity of the Slice House, 2005; its suspended swimming pool updates surrealism bringing to mind both outsize TV sets and the sharks of Damien Hirst, 1993. Re-Verse It Plaza, 2007, is enhanced by a dramatic serial use of outsized upside down flowerpot forms of varying diameter used as planters, seating, and roofscape.

A provocative program devised by the architects and their collaborators informs the Palafita Riverside Park in Porto Alegre, 2013, a PROPAR-sponsored proposal to transform a challenging infill site between a through road and an estuary, near the much-praised Museum of the Iberê Camargo Foundation by Alvaro Siza. Palafita project is a witty take on the very British counterpoint between picturesque garden and neoclassical stately house — as modified by Brazilians Burle Marx and Oscar Niemeyer working for an American client in California. The Tremaine House, 1947, reiterates the opposition and complementariness between curves (conventionally standing for organism, nature, handcraft, instinct, irrationality, willfulness) and the straight line (conventionally standing for culture, mechanism, industry, reason, artifice), but it also suggests their identity according to point of view, pointing to a transformational logic linking them. The scheme comprises five functional sectors, each displaying a characteristic repetitive pattern, the contrast between them played in many ways. Procter-Rihl work with positional, dimensional and configurational changes to reinforce their identity and organise movement, creating a rich tapestry with strict means. Contrasting utilitarian buffer sectors by the road are divided by straight arrays. The tree nurseries to the north are accommodated in parallel spaced rows of elongated rectangular greenhouses that stretch perpendicular to the road and appear as boxes covered with diverse kinds of folded roofs, enlivening the view from the neighboring hill across the road. The water filtering ponds to the south are obliquely oriented to the road making up a progression of trapezoids. Contrast by opposition emphasises the relaxed yet exuberant nature recreational sector by the river. Frankly curvilinear, it contains circular pools for the fish hatcheries scattered among the convolutions of the bike and pedestrian paths raised on stilts, riding over the land as sedate versions of roller coasters.

Procter-Rihl's formal concerns serve them well. Although much of their work to date is at the residential scale, they have developed a methodology of design across scales and disciplines. They are adroitly manipulated to address singular and repetitive programmes as well as concrete and abstract situations.

Urban Weave Housing, p 102, Moscow, competition entry, 2010.

Study for Planters for the ReVerse it Garden, p 74, competition, 2004.

Tremaine House garden by Burle Marx.

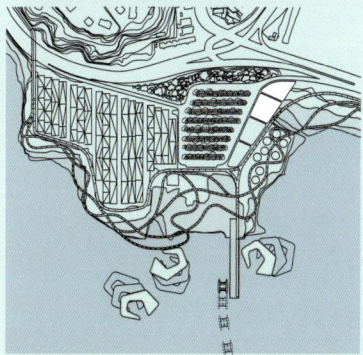
Palafita Park, p 94, production and leisure programmes woven together, 2013.

1. Kubler, George, *The Shape of Time*, New Haven and London: Yale University Press, 1962, p 6.
2. PROPAR — Programa de Pós-graduação em Arquitetura (Graduate Program in Architecture), Universidade Federal do Rio Grande do Sul, Porto Alegre, Brasil.

Marcus Field
Structure Lines
<u>Furniture, Products and other Stuff</u>

Prion Pables, p 69, 1996.

Large Strata paneling project explores transparency and overlays, p 68, 1996.

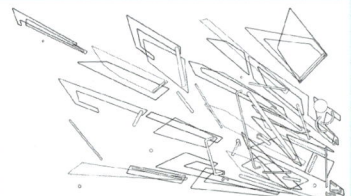

Production Drawing for the development for Zaha Hadid Blueprint Pavillion panels, 1995.

Panels for the Zaha Hadid Blueprint Pavillion, 1995.

Marcus Field is a journalist who writes about art and design for a range of newspapers and magazines, including *The Independent* and the *London Evening Standard*. He studied Art History at university and has worked as the arts editor of *The Independent on Sunday*, editor of *Blueprint* magazine, and buildings editor of *The Architects' Journal*. He is the author of two books: *Lofts*, 1998, and *Future Systems*, 1999.

Marcus Field: How did you meet and start designing together?

Fernando Rihl: We met at the Architectural Association in London in 1992. Chris had studied there and I came to do a second post-grad course, a PhD on Environment and Energy Studies.

Chris Procter: We started working together in 1995. Our first project was Bento Box, (p 88) a penthouse in Soho. A friend of mine from New Zealand commissioned us to do the flat and furniture. That's how the Ozone table (p 63) started, we made it first for his flat and then launched it at the first 100% Design Show in September 1995.

MF: Tell me more about the first tables you designed?

FR: We were working a lot with acrylic at the time, specially live-edge acrylic. Acrylic was a familiar material known to us for architectural model making, although live-edge acrylic was a fairly new material on the market mostly used for signage. We were the first designers to use live edge in furniture production and people would associate our work with the material. Acrylic became our obssesion then. We researched acrylic suppliers everywhere we went. We had seven different suppliers from all over the world to get a wider range of colours and hues. We used this varied colour range in order to mix and match different unique combinations. In some cases, the industry would make a special colour for us or we bought left overs from one-off orders. Satin finish was not available on the market at that time, so we had to hand sand the sheets to achieve that soft hazy effect.

CP: 100% Design was just being launched in London. I remember we signed up two weeks before the show in August 1995. Fernando had been designing furniture for his retail projects in Brazil. His knowledge of welding led us to work with steel and acrylic. We showed the Ozone and Prion tables (pp 63 and 68) both with live-edge acrylic and steel structure at that year. The trend at the time was minimal, natural, dark wood, no colour and no pattern. Our pieces stood out. At that show, Zaha Hadid saw the Prion Tables and commissioned us to make 3 m by 2 m panels for a *Blueprint* magazine/ Elementer ironmongery exhibition pavilion in 1995. The Ozone and Prion tables were widely published that year.

FR: The heavy steel base Prion tables made in 1995 were replaced by the Strata tables the following year (p 66) using a very lightweight aluminium plastic composite material base. In that year 1996, we also launched the Prion boxes (p 69) for the Japanese market and Topo shelving (p 104) in 6 mm thick blue translucent plastic and birch ply. We only did two prototypes of the Topo shelving for the show in 1996. The pieces went straight to a Bonhams Contemporay Furniture auction called Futures. The following year, we developed the shelving as a production piece in 12 mm.

MF: And so did it become a business for you?

FR: Yes, we had the Strata table in 17 colour variations in 1996. In the beginning, we sold at Collette in Paris and about five design shops and galleries around London. A couple of years later after exhibiting in Melbourne, Tokyo, and New York we were selling everywhere around the world from Sydney Design Museum to MoMA (NYC), Gubi in Denmark, E&Y in Tokyo, Cream (Singapore), Totem (NYC), Milan, Cologne, San Francisco. We also sold pieces as props for films like *Lost in Space*, for example. Special commissions appeared for British Embassy, Joyce Shop (HK), British Embassy, Blueprint Pavilion, London Fashion Week and so on.

MF: So you were producers, manufacturers, everything?

CP: Yes, like most British designers at that time it was the way to work. When we started, Cool Britannia was on a high. It was a very interesting time in London. We joined a group of designers — Inflate, Jane Atfield, Michael Marriot, Michael Young, Azumis, JAM… who also produced their own things following the example of Tom Dixon and Ron Arad. Our first pieces in 1995 and 1996 were made in a small workshop in North London. They were all hand-cut. As we got more orders in 1997 we found bigger production companies in the UK and started to use computer CNC routing for the Space Lily bowl and the new Topo shelving. The process was fairly new, not that available for plastic, and we had to convince them to work for us.

Flow shelving, p 107, at the British Design Exhibition, Château Bosmelet, France, 1998.

MF: Do you still produce your pieces in this way?

FR: Not anymore. We acquired a lot of experience engaging in production and distribution but we prefer to concentrate on designing and working directly with industry now. However, we still develop prototype pieces in a speculative way. It is an on-going process. We never stop testing new ideas and engaging with new methods of making. We have a partnership with a company in Brazil who manage our production pieces and develop new prototypes for us. We learn a lot from speculative projects which feed back into our practice.

Nest Sofa, p 110, 2000.

MF: Would you say that your furniture has its roots in Modernist principles?

CP: Yes, there is that sense of clarity, and we don't hide elements. That's very modernist. But there is something that's also a bit more current, more complex, with elements of distortion, perspective, and pattern. Also we like to work on local design solutions and not necessarily impose a Modernist style.

MF: You mention handmaking—are you interested in craft?

FR: Yes we are very interested in craft but it has to have a new take. There has to be a level of innovation and originality when working with an established technology and traditional methods. The Tupi chairs (p 40), for example, came about after exploring different weaving techniques and effects in Brazil. Our Nest sofa was another way to investigate weave (p 110) which was presented at Salone Satelite Milan in 2000. *Abitare* magazine called it a tridimensional carpet as a new seating typology. And Massimo Morozzi, at the time design director of Edra, was very interested in the concept of a sofa without structure. Massimo had previously purchased some of our pieces from the Colette shop in Paris.

Prion Box / Topo Shelving, 1996.

MF: Tell me more about the Tupi chair; it has such an unusual shape.

FR: The Tupi chair is a hybrid of two cultures, the Austrian and the Tupi. Tupi is a southern Brazilian Indigenous group that develops beautiful very colourful woven artefacts. The project fuses toguether two different weaving techniques. Traditionally the Thonet woven chair is woven on a flat plane creating a consistent and continuous weave thoughtout. What is innovative in this project is the continuous organic steel frame that distorts the weaving in different ways.

Prion Box, p 69, colour variations, 1996.

It blurs the familiar. Using two colours of cane picks out this distortion and emphasises the individual line of weave rather than a continuous surface. The references come from things we have experienced.

MF: Is there anything particularly Brazilian in your work?

FR: Our references come from objects or situations we have previously experienced. The Topo shelving for example was inspired by the Brazilian shading devices when I was researching daylighting and louvre systems for my PhD. Brazilian design is generally more craft and wood-based than our work. We are interested in digital aesthetics with an ethereal quality, weightlessness and structural delicacy.

MF: What do you think of furniture which is made and sold as art, at art prices?

CP: I have real problems with that. There is no shame in something that works well. We aim for a balance between the functional and the conceptual object. I tend to think a lot of art furniture is just visual and not very functional as it goes to the realm of sculpture and fine art installation. Design is both a functionally- and conceptually-based discipline.

MF: Is your work affected by trends or fashion?

FR: Yes, if you define fashion as an expression of the times. We don't resist fashion but we always explore our own take on it. I think the aim is to develop something that has the spirit of the moment to come but it is at the same time unique and challenging. But we are not interested in trends. Permanence and longetivity are very important for us.

MF: Do you work as a team; design things together or separately?

CP: Everything we design is designed together; the process is very fluid and natural as we have been working together for a long time. Having a partnership means you always have another critical eye to keep you on track.

MF: You have talked about how you are interested in the contrast between the familiar and the extraordinary. How does this manifest itself in your work?

FR: The extraordinary is developed through digital aesthetics, a synthetic colour sensibility and geometric complexity. The familiar is either by an established local typology, making technique or local material. In the Tupi chair for example the familiar element is the woven cane seat; the unfamiliar is the geometry and its continuous frame. That is the original and unique element in that piece. The continuous frame starts to interfere with the pattern and the familiar element and is thus, slowly abstracted. If we work with symbols, the digital aesthetics will interefere with them, making them suggestive and less obvious.

MF: How do you come up with the terms—fold, perforate, float and weave—that you use to categorise your work?

FR: There are some design actions that keep reappearing in our work. These design actions are verbs loaded with spatial qualities. They either represent an interest in surfaces or suggest a digital sensibility of weightlessness. Early development of this publication started with eight action verbs but we decided to focus on the actions that kept being reinterpreted in our work. This publication presents our work not in terms of a linear timeline, scale or discipline but under an operative system. It is a more revealing and interactive strategy. And we hope readers will engage with our process and find new links we have not seen.

Strap Chair, p 100, Study for tall version.

Gallaccio Bed headboard, 2006.

Exploring weave distortions Tupi, p 40.

Do not Push table component.

Christopher Procter, Fernando Rihl

Operational System

Design Manoeuvers and Spatial Verbs

This book illustrates a method of how we explore formal and spatial concerns in our design process. The method is grounded on linguistics based on spatial verbs, verbs that embrace strong spatial qualities and suggest formal interventions. These verbs are categorised as actions or design manoeuvers, as we have called them. The method had been originally suggested in 1967 by the artist Richard Serra with his 84 verb compilation. Conditional design methods, where the variables are limited by a set of parameters set up at the beginning of the project have been extensively explored by parametric and digital architecture which deliver complex and extra-ordinary architecture but often as completely non-contextual formal pursuits.

The studio aims to bring place and identity by weaving symbols and archetypes to the liguistic method, an approach called TransLocal where the local and the global fuse together as previously discussed in our essay on page 8. Our method highlights intrinsic connections to place and identity, key elements in the production of architecture. It is an investigation of linguistics with anthropological dimensions fusing spatial verbs to local archetypes, symbols, signs and signifiers. The aim is to deliver an architecture that is culturally responsive but, at the same time, forward thinking by embracing digital techniques in the investigation of space. The implementation of digital complexity to familiar symbols and archetypes camouflages their meaning and brings an interpretative process with a world of suggestions which makes the decoding process a longer, richer experience. The ultimate goal is to generate an architecture that responds to place with unique and original architecture.

Some projects are more figurative than others depending on permanence, context or scale. The "actions or design manoeuvers" are our firestarters to our spatial investigations which are synchronised with other design criteria such as, context, spatial experience, orientation, programme, typology, meaning, signs, symbols and archetypes. These actions set the boundaries where our design manoeuvres can be tested and investigated. The method attracts us as it embraces a diagrammatic purity that will inevitably be reflected in our designs.

Our studio employs this method as continual process of rewriting and reinterpreting spatial verbs in different scales, programmes or disciplines. Key design manoeuvres, such as fold, perforate, float and weave, are regularly revisited in our studio. Any main action will be connected to a secondary action in order to fully respond to the brief requirements. It generates this way to a hybrid action such as slice/engrave, slice/extend, slice/extrude, slice/shift and slice/wrap, for example. These hybrid actions become complementary operations in this operative system. For the purpose of categorisation in this book, we name the key action that embraces the main concept in each project.

to roll	to curve
to crease	to lift
to fold	to inlay
to store	to impress
to bend	to fire
to shorten	to flood
to twist	to smear
to dapple	to rotate
to crumple	to swirl
to shave	to support
to tear	to hook
to chip	to suspend
to split	to spread
to cut	to hang
to sever	to collect
to drop	of tension
to remove	of gravity
to simplify	of entropy
to differ	of nature
to disarrange	of grouping
to open	of layering
to mix	of felting
to splash	to grasp
to knot	to tighten
to spill	to bundle
to droop	to heap
to flow	to gather

to scatter	to modulate
to arrange	to distill
to repair	of waves
to discard	of electromagnetic
to pair	of inertia
to distribute	of ionization
to surfeit	of polarization
to complement	of refraction
to enclose	of simultaneity
to surround	of tides
to encircle	of reflection
to hide	of equilibrium
to cover	of symmetry
to wrap	of friction
to dig	to stretch
to tie	to bounce
to bind	to erase
to weave	to spray
to join	to systematize
to match	to refer
to laminate	to force
to bond	of mapping
to hinge	of location
to mark	of context
to expand	of time
to dilute	of carbonization
to light	to continue

Richard Serra, *Verb List*, 1967–1968. Graphite on paper, 2 sheets, each 10 x 8" (25.4 x 20.3cm). The Museum of Modern Art, New York. Gift of the artist in honor of Wynn Kramarsky. © 2011 Richard Serra/Artists Rights Society (ARS), New York, DIGITAL IMAGE © The Museum of Modern Art/Scala, Florence.

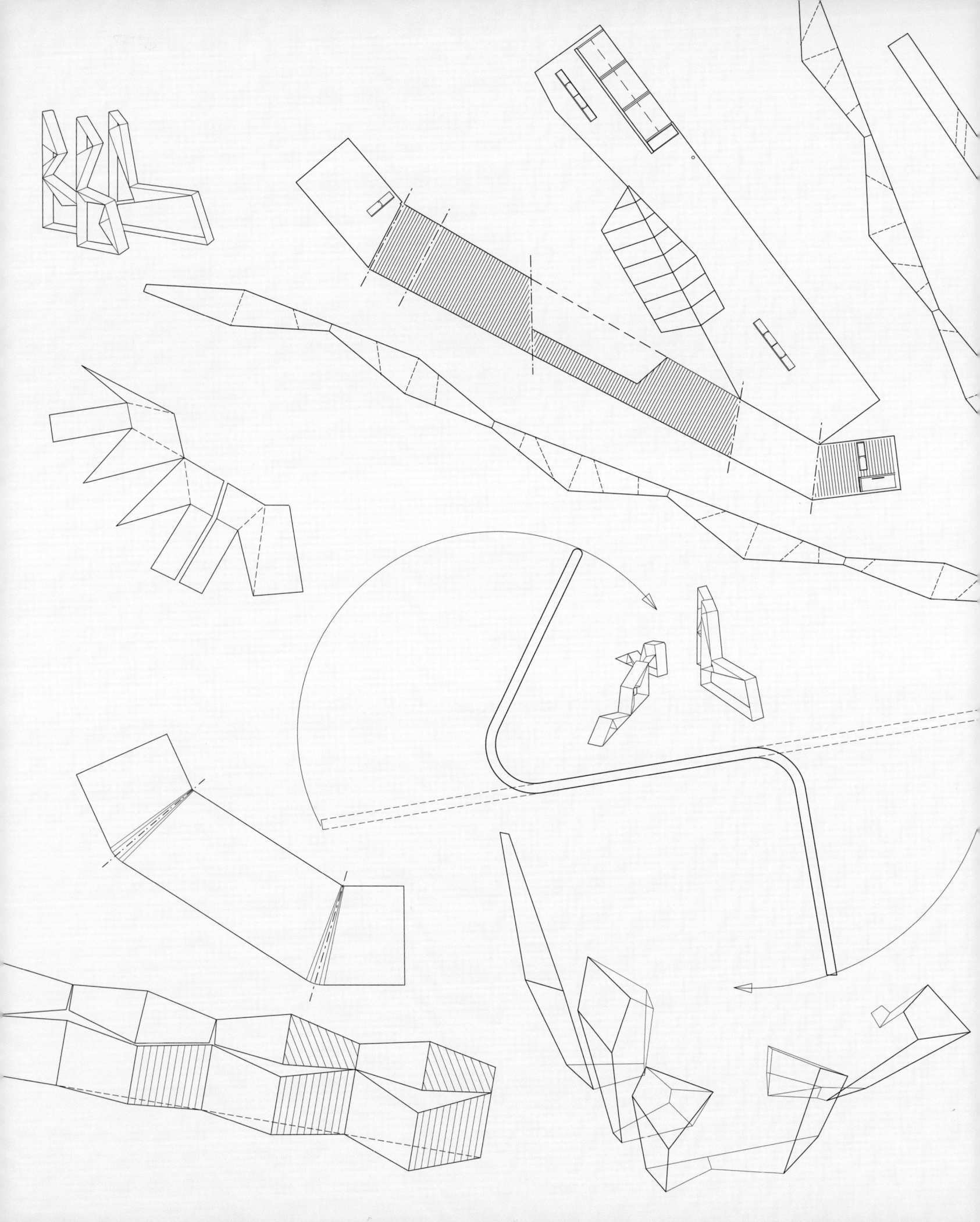

Fold

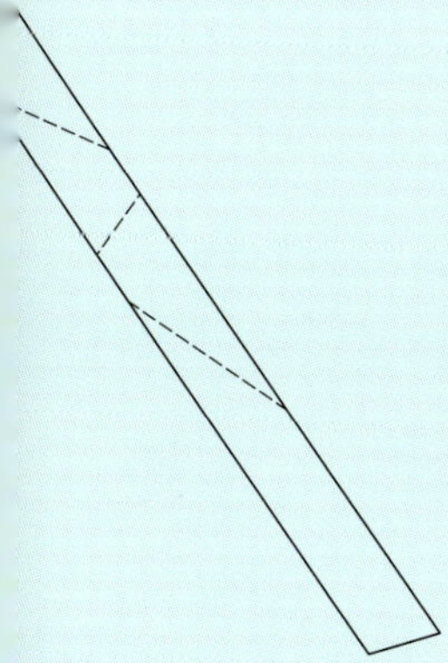

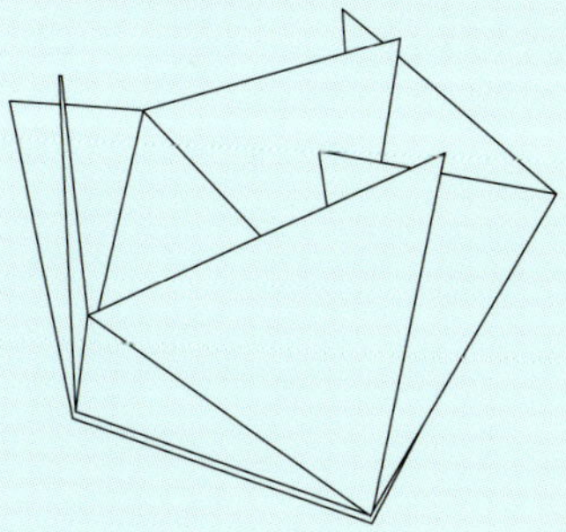

Fold is an action that is immediately associated with interventions to planes or surfaces. Surfaces interest us as they embrace etheral qualities such as structural lightness and sense of weightlessness, constant elements in our work. The projects shown in this chapter emphasise an envelope defined by planes and surfaces suggesting a paper quality.

The exploration of folding in architecture has generated spatial complexity questioning the traditional notion of orthogonal environments impacting on how we perceive space today. Deleuze's concept of a continuous smooth seamless space interests us mostly from a phenomenological perspective. Folded structures inevitably create spatial illusions as they blur the planes we inhabit. Space becomes richer when decoding these complex geometries by the constant challenge to our perception. We investigate complexity with a restrained viewpoint exploring its relation to motion, the body and the senses.

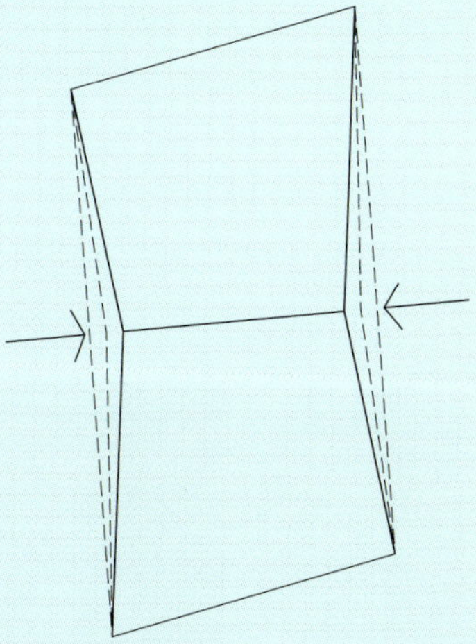

Our studio seeks a balance where excitement does not become overpowering and autocratic. Spatial distortions are not random formal exercises but connected to other factors that the users will discover as they engage deeper with the projects in this book. Fold is usually explored in our work with complementary actions such as to slice, to pull, to extend, to stretch, to chop, etc.

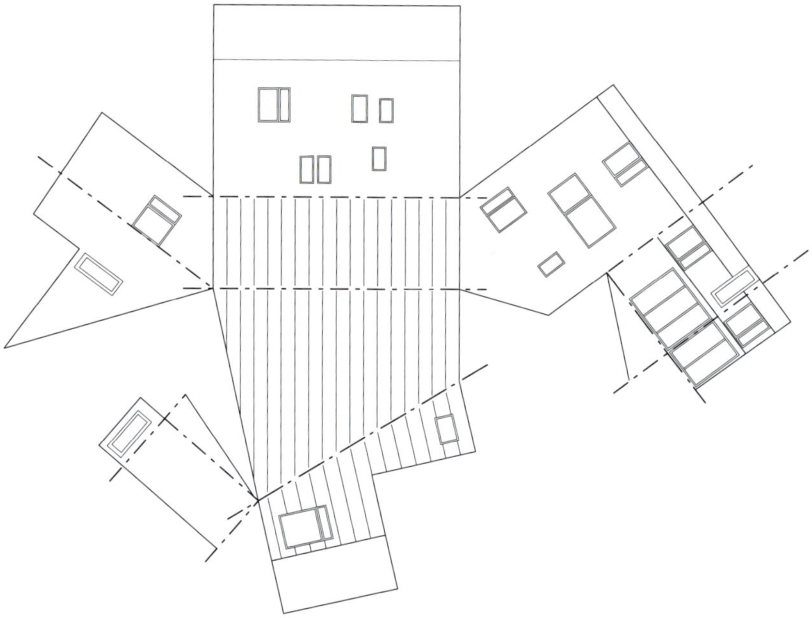

Winter, from west hill showing New England "saltbox" house shape typology.

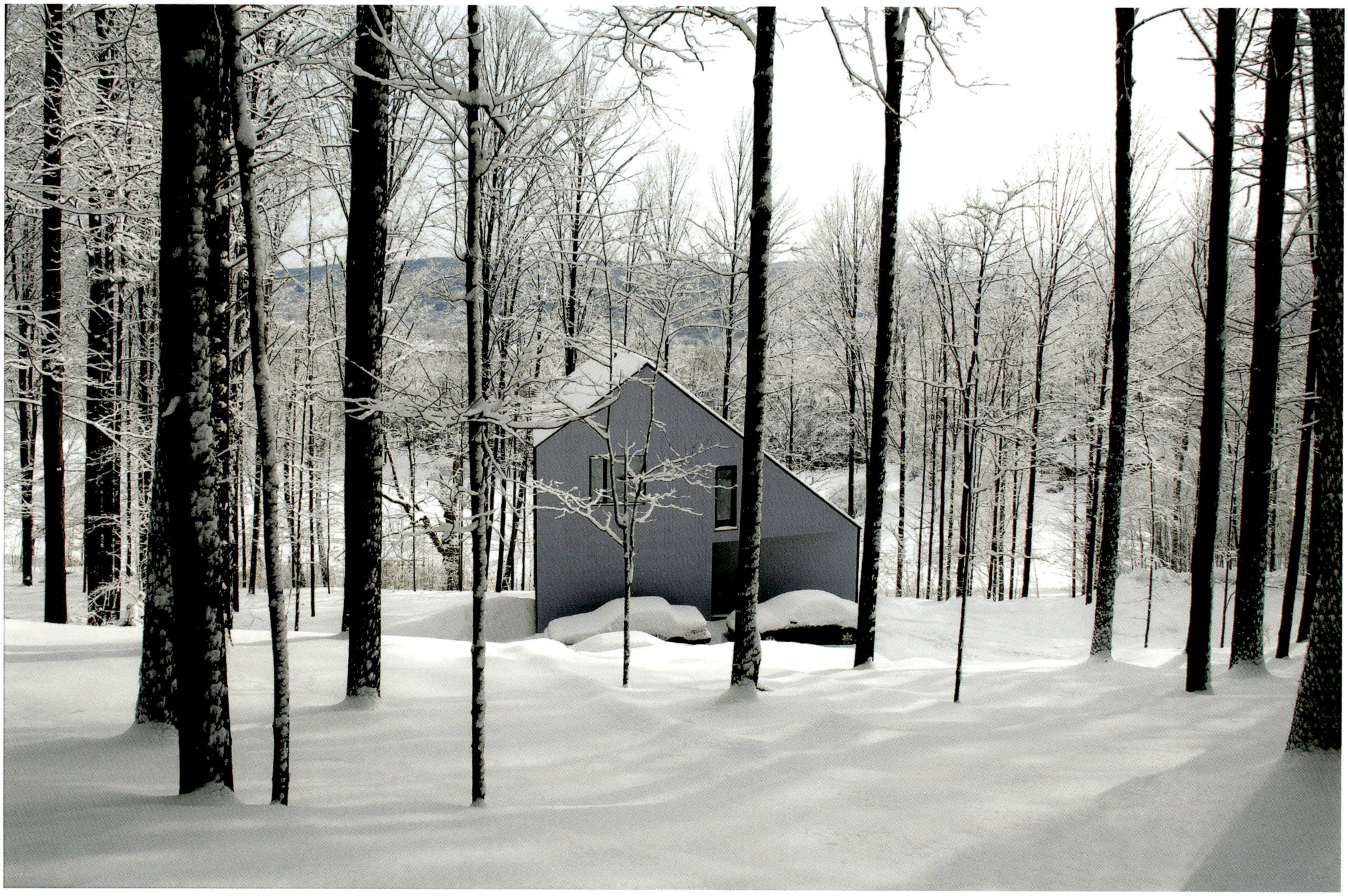

Private Client, Brattleboro, Vermont USA
Pull House
rural sustainable house, 2008

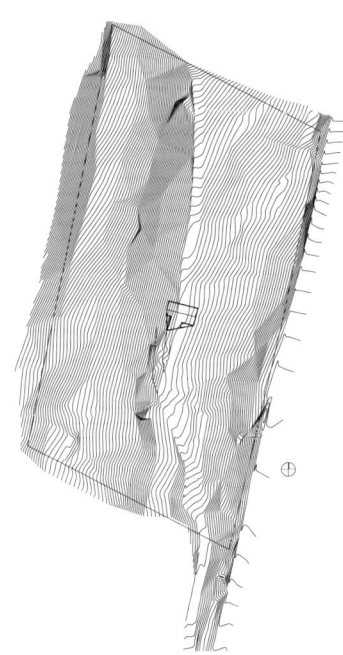

Pull House explores the familiar through the exploration of local typologies and building technology. The prismatic aesthetics merge with the local barn typology creating uniqueness and eccentricity to the project. On the public road, one can see the traditional barn, but as one approaches on the private drive, the house reveals itself with a contemporary folded aesthetic. The roof oriented to the south for future solar panels sheds snow away from the main entrance.

  The client, required an accessible disabled-friendly house. The ground entry floor is stepless, with living, dining, kitchen, bedroom, and wetroom shower bathroom. This level has flush floor details for free wheelchair entry to all spaces particularly the tiled shower wetroom. The upper floor consists of two further bedrooms, two bathrooms and a mezzanine loft overlooking the living room. The walkout basement contains a mechanical room, laundry space along with another bedroom, bathroom, and large game room. The house volume is energy efficient, close to the ideal spherical shape, with a low surface area and a small footprint.

  The typical Vermont landscape is defined by rural wooded mountains with scattered farms and clearings. Nearby buildings are simple pitched roof timber houses and barns. The site borders the Kipling Estate where Rudyard Kipling built a linear shingle style house where he lived for four years and wrote *The Jungle Book*, *Seven Seas*, and *Captain Courageous*.

Folded Geometry: Simplicity and Complexity

Simple distortions are juxtaposed to the north side of the building which appears quite ordinary. From the gable ends one can see in the building a vernacular "saltbox" form or an extended roof with a changed pitch neither of which are true. Its aesthetic is a precise prism with flush details and triangular spaces due to the exploration of the oblique on the south facade. A simple pitched roof "barn" has had one corner pulled out and moved diagonally from its rectangular loci. This has folded the entry gable facade from the ridge and created a strong diagonal south facade. The roof, a local standing seam metal surface folds down away towards west to redirect snow away from the main entrance. Internally, the folded geometry creates a dramatic double-height living room where a low window frames the long private road. Windows are positioned judiciously to extend views out to the landscape. The folded gable west entry facade is painted a contrasting colour to accent its difference. The east and north facades are clad with rough timber coloured to look like old weathered "barn boards" and random openings.

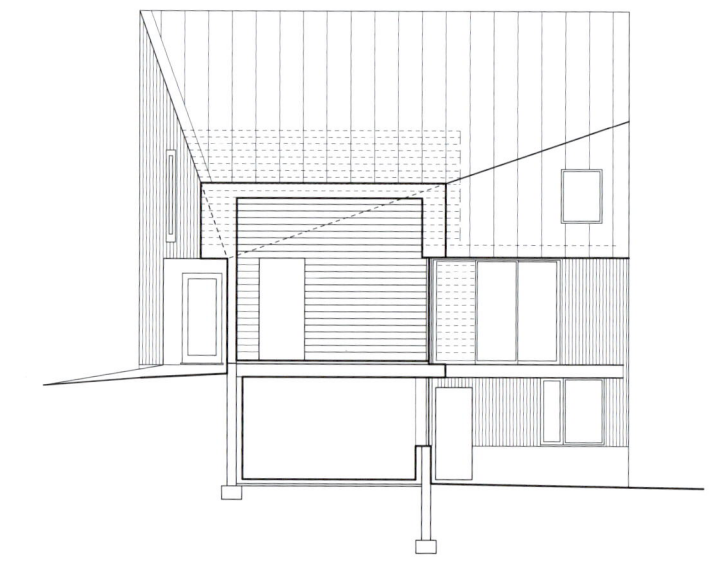

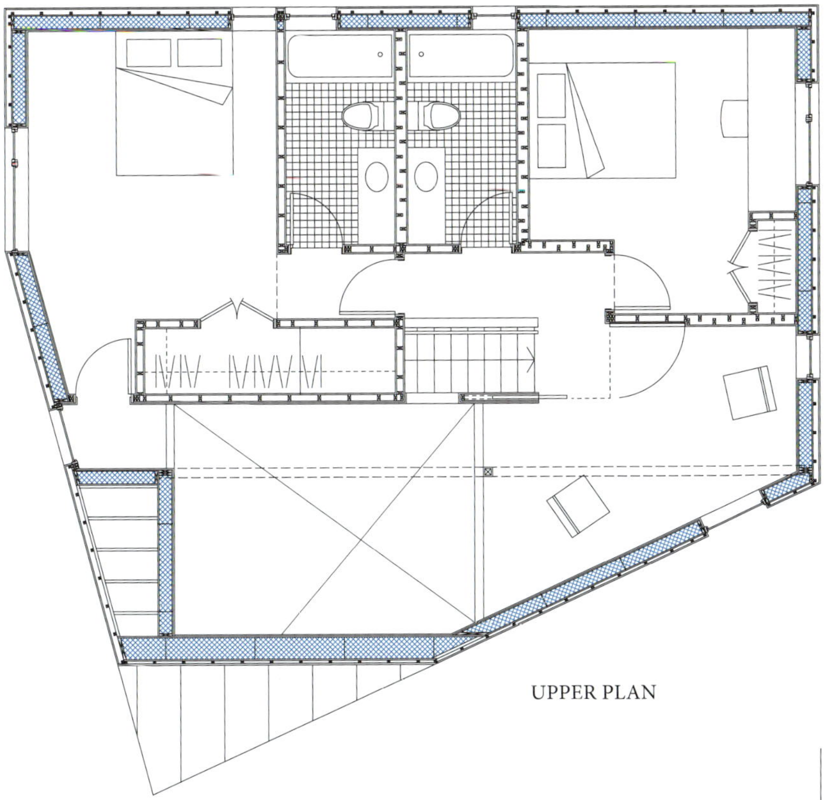

UPPER PLAN

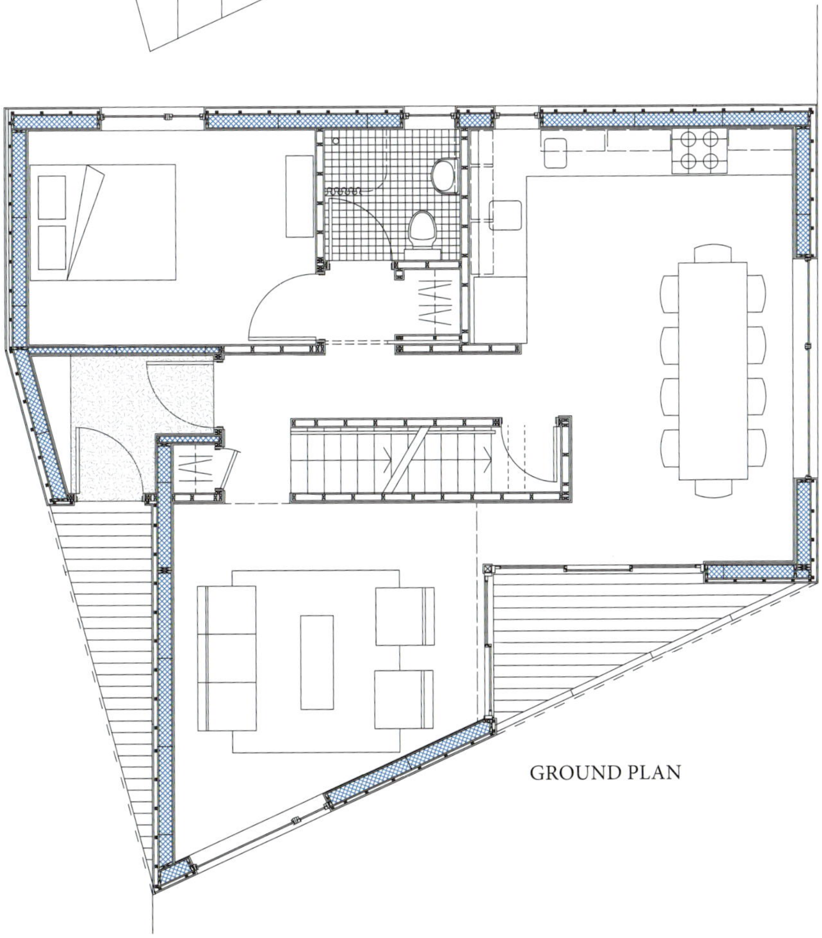

GROUND PLAN

Complex geometry at the corner where ceiling and walls meet due to external roof folding.

The northeast "traditional barn" facade in contrast to the faceted contemporary aesthetics. The wood panelled interior picks up on Shaker or Amish cultures and their pure and understated design aesthetics.

The low window in the living room frames the garden. The loft space becomes a guest room when closed off with sliding and hinged two full-height door panels.

Individual timber planks were dyed in brown, black, purple, creating a tension between the natural and the synthetic. A warm pink polished concrete floor for absorption of solar gain and thermal mass complements the living space.

The design employs MMC modern methods of construction in a customised design. The house was erected in eight days from factory prefabricated components.

Day two — First wall

Day two — Living room walls

Day four — upper floor walls

Day seven — roof truss blocks

Day seven — fixing trusses

Day eight — 12 inch (300 mm) Sips Living room roof

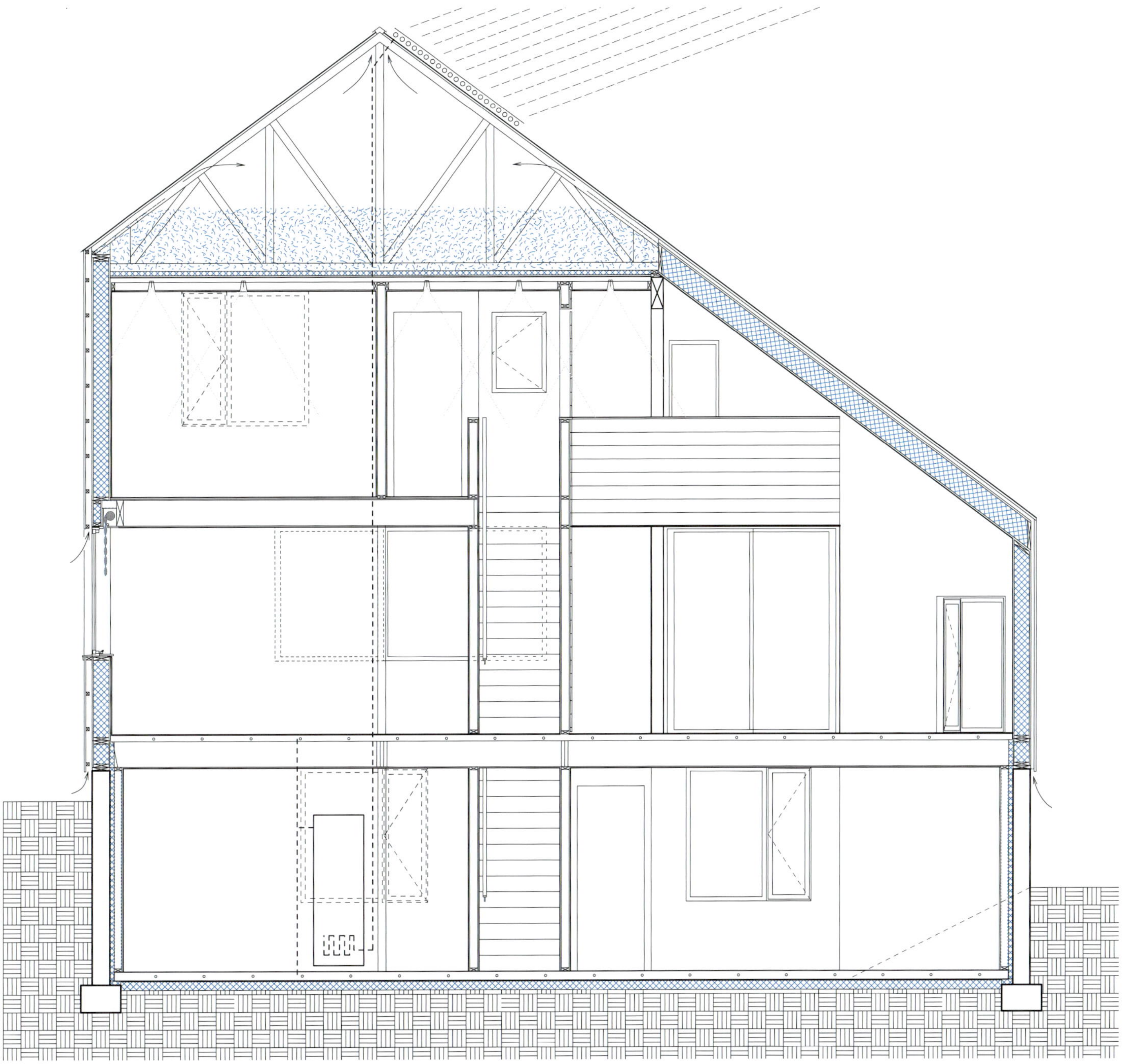

Passivhaus and Other Sustainable Features

The house employs Passivhaus principles such as compact volume, triple-glazed windows, air to air heat recovery ventilation, low infiltration sealed construction, and high levels of insulation. The roof loft has blown cellulose with european U values of 0.08W/m2K (USA is R-70), SIPS walls are european U values of 0.142W/m2K (USA is R-40). Minimal additional heat is supplied to basement and ground in radiant concrete floors from electric and future solar panels. Windows are triple-glazed with provision for thermal quilt blinds. The house employs Structural Insulated Panels technology or SIPS, a familiar and popular local technology since the late 70s right after the first Oil Crisis. These are stress skin panels where the structural loading is born by the 12 mm Oriented Strand Boards (OSB) skins on the dense extruded polystyrene (XEPS) foam core of the panel. Good U/R values are achievable as there is no timber cold bridge through the wall except around window frames or corners. Walls and roof are vented behind the cladding to prevent condensation build up on the OSB skin.

Customising a foam panel on site with special saw.

Private Client, Highbury, London, UK
Mansard House
new urban house / artists studios, 2014

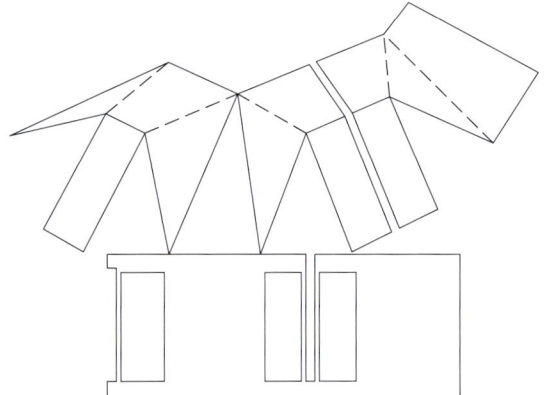

Mansard explores the familiar in a typical English Victorian housing terrace in a conservation area in Highbury, London. The brief was for a residence to complete the terrace height line and to rebuild studios in rear yard industrial sheds. These studios, accessible by a tunnel under the Victorian Terrace, use faceted sawtooth clerestories for good daylighting. Two approaches were considered, demolition and rebuild of the garage or recladding and reuse, which in the end was more sustainable. The reusing employs the concept of an oversized two storey mansard with windows matching the terrace scale. Folding dormer side flanks bring a new prismatic quality. Rather than traditional slate, the mansard is clad with oversize handmade pewter coloured tiles similar in tone to slate, but with an iridescent shimmering metallic effect. The front facade of blue engineered bricks is recessed into the old garage doorway creating a protected entry, which retains the memory of the former garage. The main living space retains half of the former industrial space with its steel trusses.

Existing garage to remodel.

Rear studios with sawtooth industrial top clerestorey windows.

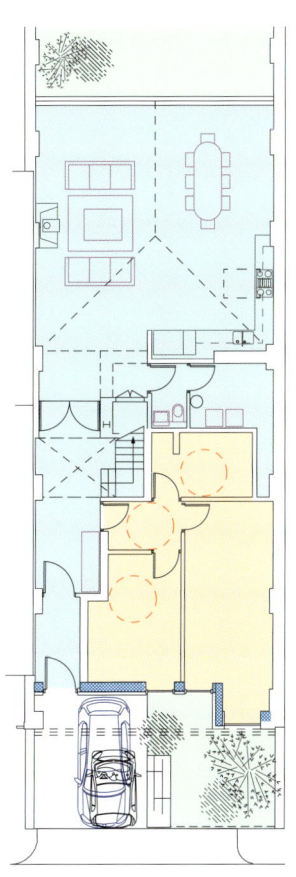

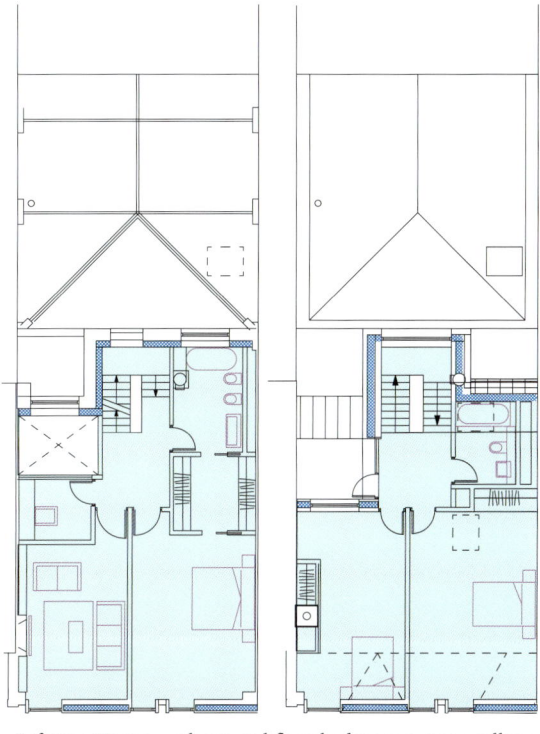

Lifetime Homes with ground floor bedroom suite in yellow. Wheelchair turning circles shown and a wider wheelchair acessible parking /off loading bay. Retrofit heavy insulation shown in blue hatching on existing walls and new roof.

GROUND   FIRST   SECOND

London, UK
Accordion Terrace
new sustainable development, 2013

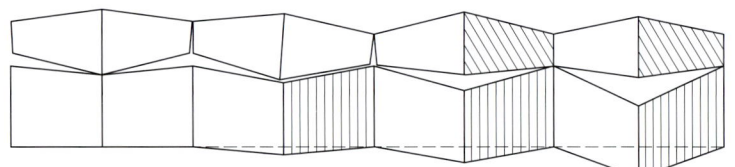

Accordion investigates the British terrace house typology and proposes a new prototype, adaptable to different orientations. The facade is animated with its alternating projecting bay windows and recessed entry disabled parking. Its mansard, when seen in a line, creates a playful undulation of folded roof planes. The plans provide a four bedroom family house with flexible one bedroom flat as either separate housing, or lifetime homes accommodation.

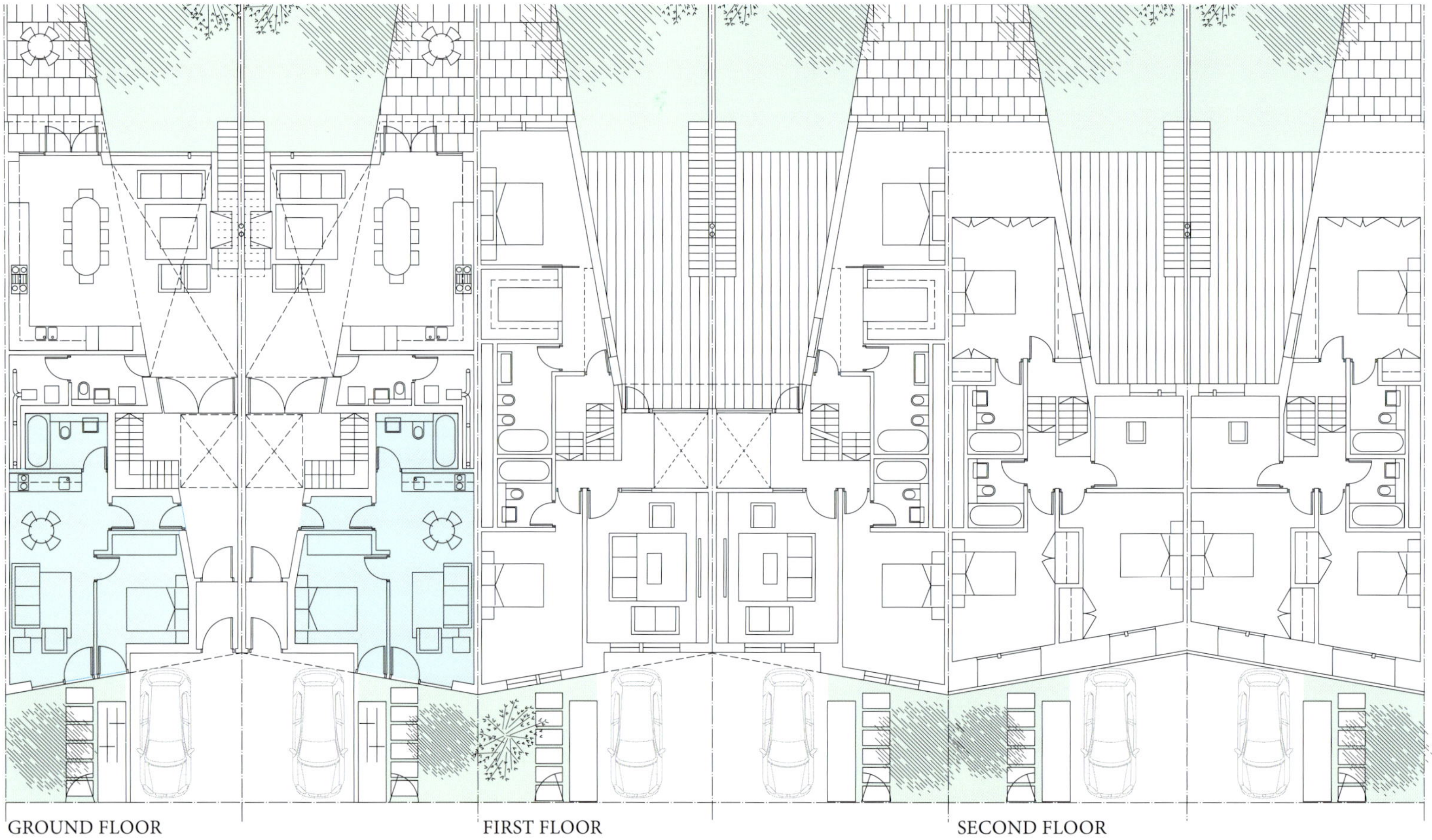

GROUND FLOOR   FIRST FLOOR   SECOND FLOOR

Previous study of rear with balcony.

Flexi-scape

exhibition London Fashion Week, 1998

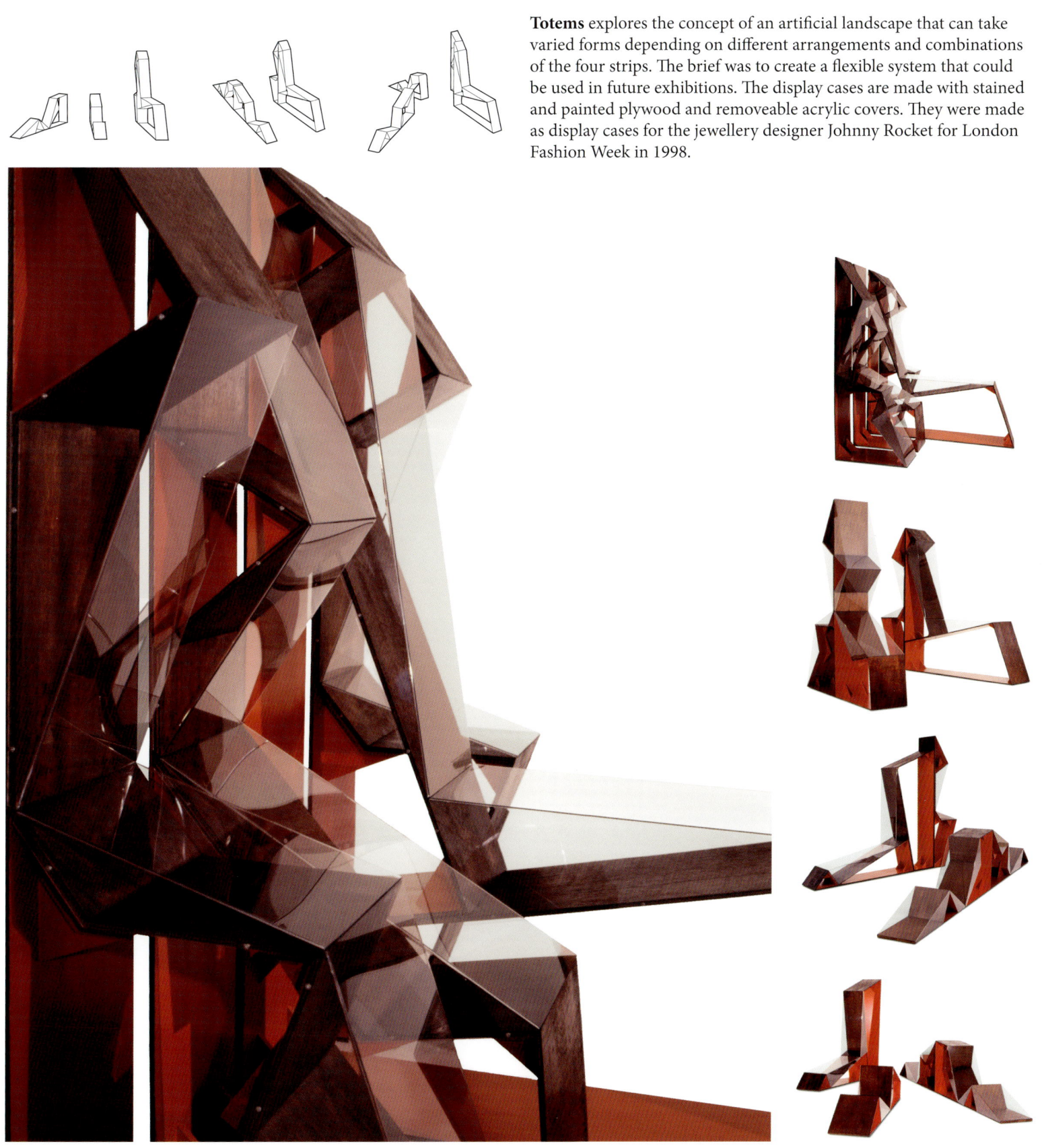

Totems explores the concept of an artificial landscape that can take varied forms depending on different arrangements and combinations of the four strips. The brief was to create a flexible system that could be used in future exhibitions. The display cases are made with stained and painted plywood and removeable acrylic covers. They were made as display cases for the jewellery designer Johnny Rocket for London Fashion Week in 1998.

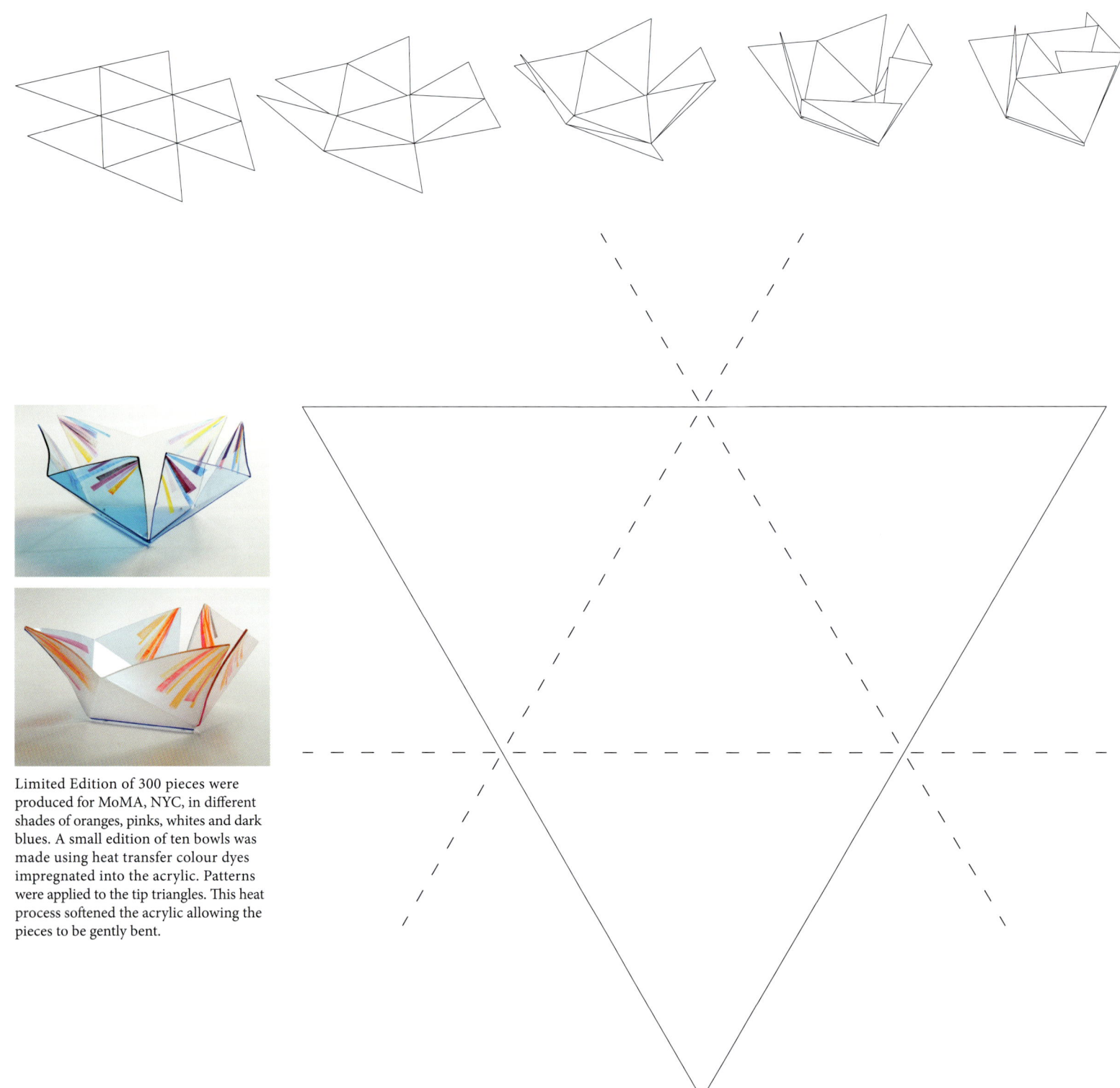

Limited Edition of 300 pieces were produced for MoMA, NYC, in different shades of oranges, pinks, whites and dark blues. A small edition of ten bowls was made using heat transfer colour dyes impregnated into the acrylic. Patterns were applied to the tip triangles. This heat process softened the acrylic allowing the pieces to be gently bent.

Space Lily Bowl

limited edition fruit bowl, 1997-1998

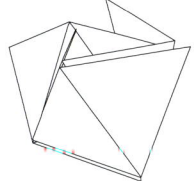 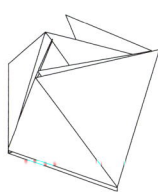 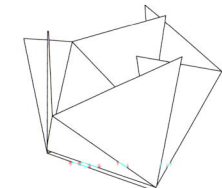 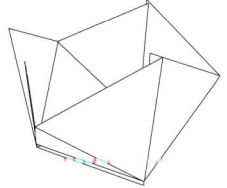 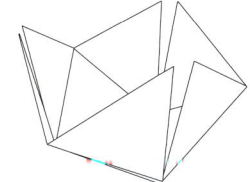

Space Lily explores the representation of movement through a folded structure. The bowl made of 3 mm acrylic unfolds like petals of a flower. These bowls were assembled randomly in different shades of blues, oranges, pinks and frost white combinations. A total of 450 limited edition pieces were made between 1997–1998. A special orange edition of 300 pieces were made for the MoMA Art Shop in 1997 and a pink edition for the Colette shop in Paris in 1998. Components were CNC cut, but folded and assembled by hand.

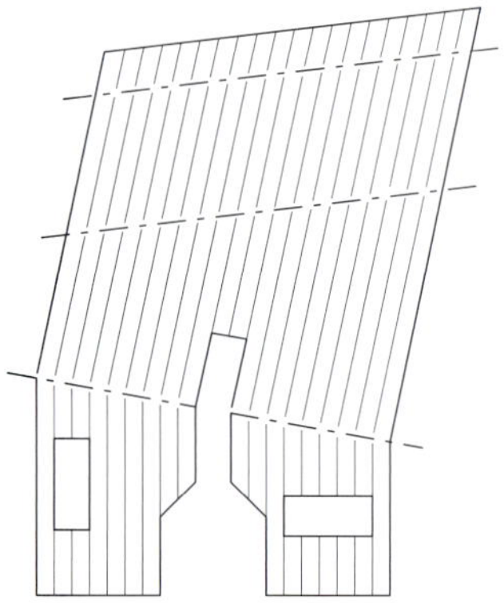

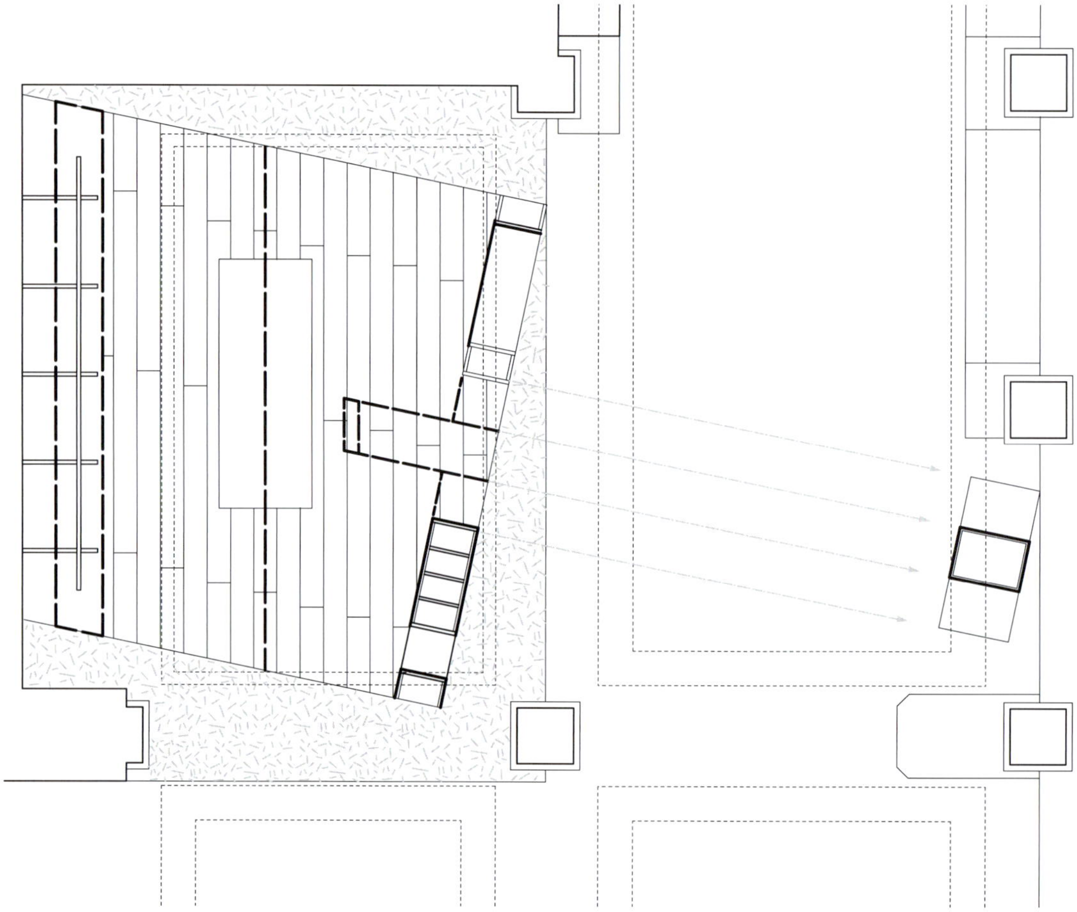

Plan shows chimney pulled out across circulation aisle as additional display unit.

Below, the thick polycarbonate walls work as a storage space for stock.

Caramel at Harrods, London, UK
Mini Me Shop

Caramel childrens clothing concession and brand, 2008

MiniMe explores the concept of the "small" or "minature" in architecture and its spatial implications. The project was commissioned by Caramel, a London based children's clothing brand. The brief was to create a flagship shop in Harrods department store in London. The design delivers an iconic piece with a strong brand identity, able to be flexible and adapt to different spatial requirements for future franchises.

The project was conceived as a giant doll's house where adults experience a miniaturised world. Some areas are adult free such as the rear of the distorted roof with lower ceiling height accessible only by children. Key building components, such as fireplace are pulled apart from the structure allowing children to access the house through the chimney. The structure adapts to the given space by distorting itself with an oblique aesthetic.

MiniMe uses the wall thickness to store stock suggesting a take on building insulation as most department stores do not provide additional space for stock. The see-through material of the walls creates an ever changing ghost effect each season reflecting the season's colour palette. The shoes are displayed on the "garden planting".

<u>Blueprint Magazine, London, UK</u>
22 Folds Stand
<u>exhibition stand, 100% Design, 1997</u>

 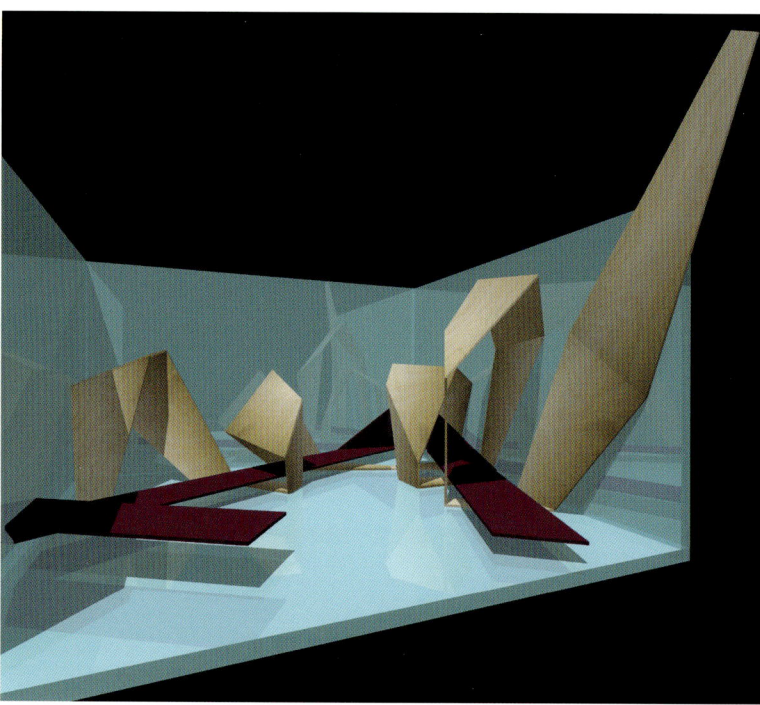

Spiral piece made from only five sheets
of birch ply with no waste. Sheet layout
pattern below, assembled as a strip above.

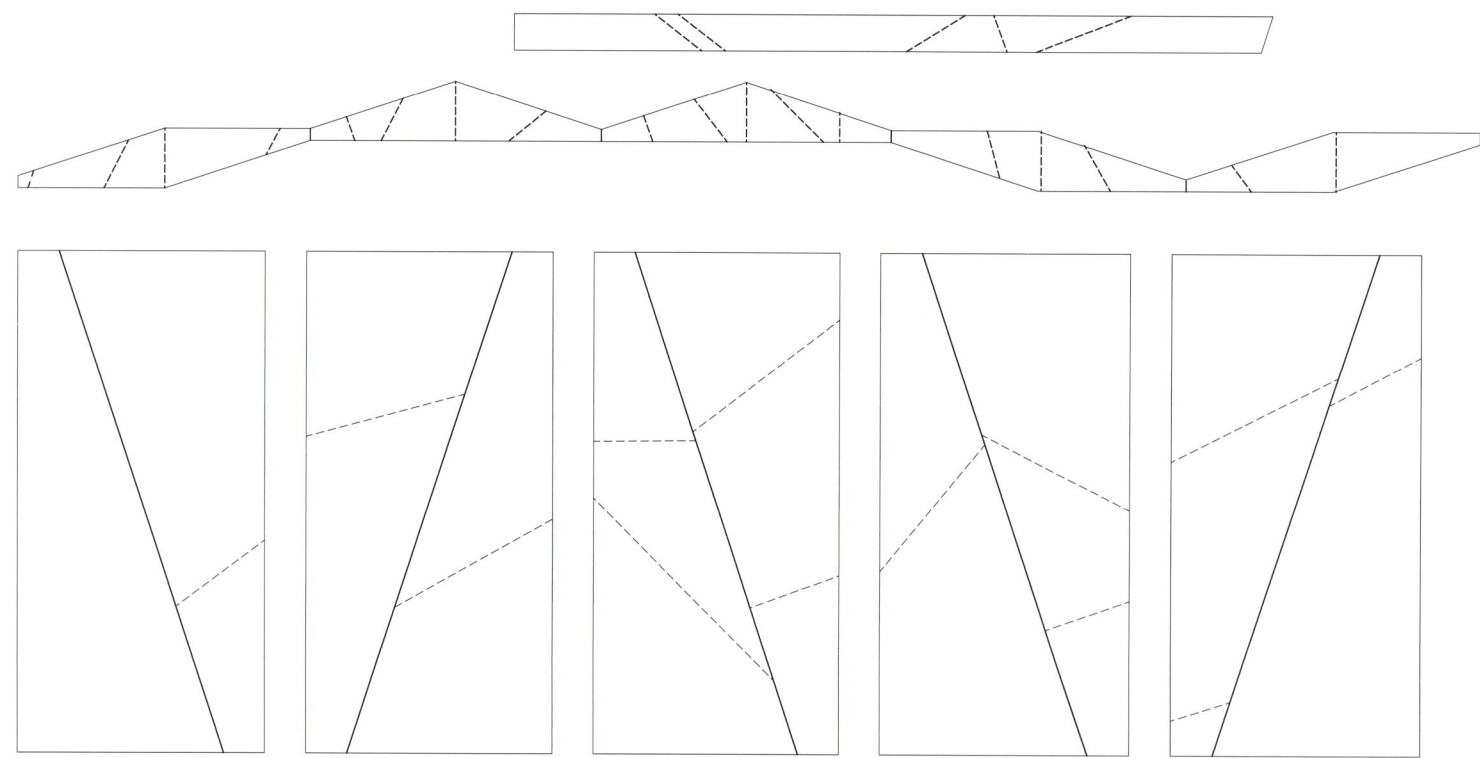

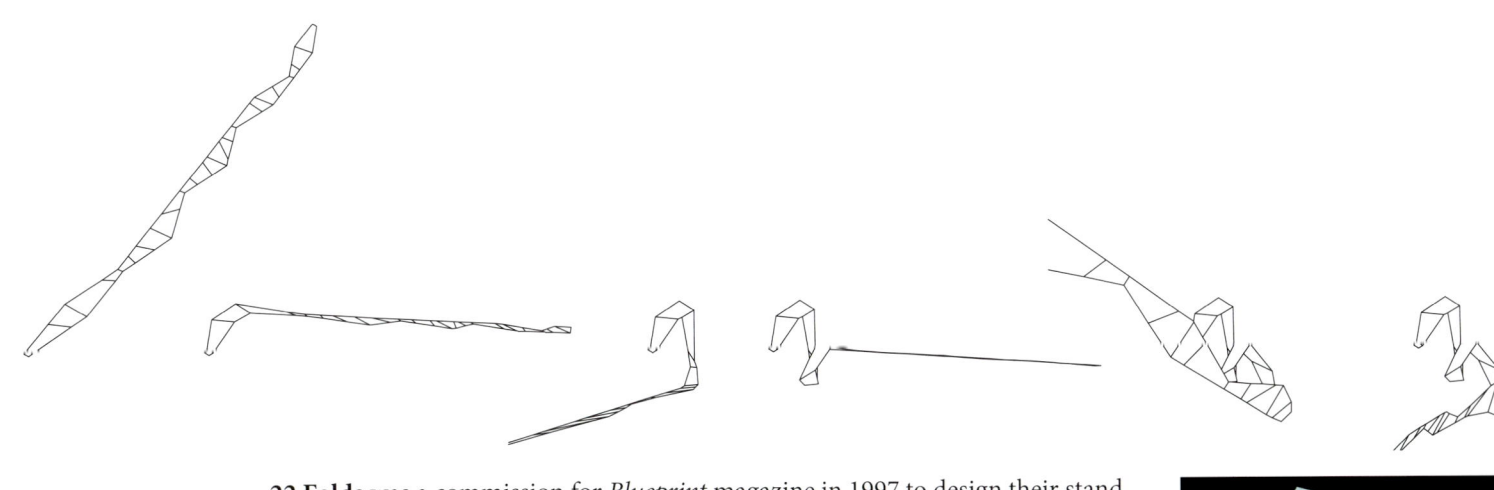

22 Folds was a commission for *Blueprint* magazine in 1997 to design their stand at 100% Design London to exhibit the finalists of a design competition. The brief was a low cost, easy, quick to assemble exhibition stand. The design strategy was to create a dynamic challenging environment that folds specifically around key pieces creating different perspectives and conversations with the objects displayed. Two bands wrap around each other creating an exciting environment to host these finalists design pieces. The structure was made of five birch plywood sheets and three Sterling Board sheets with no waste. The bands were hinged with piano hinges to achieve a minimum assembly time during construction.

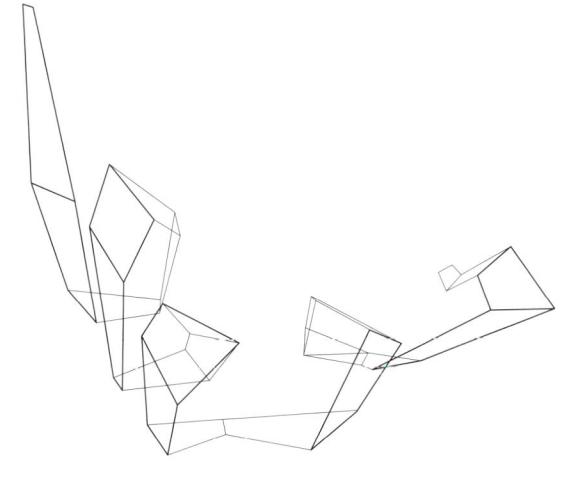

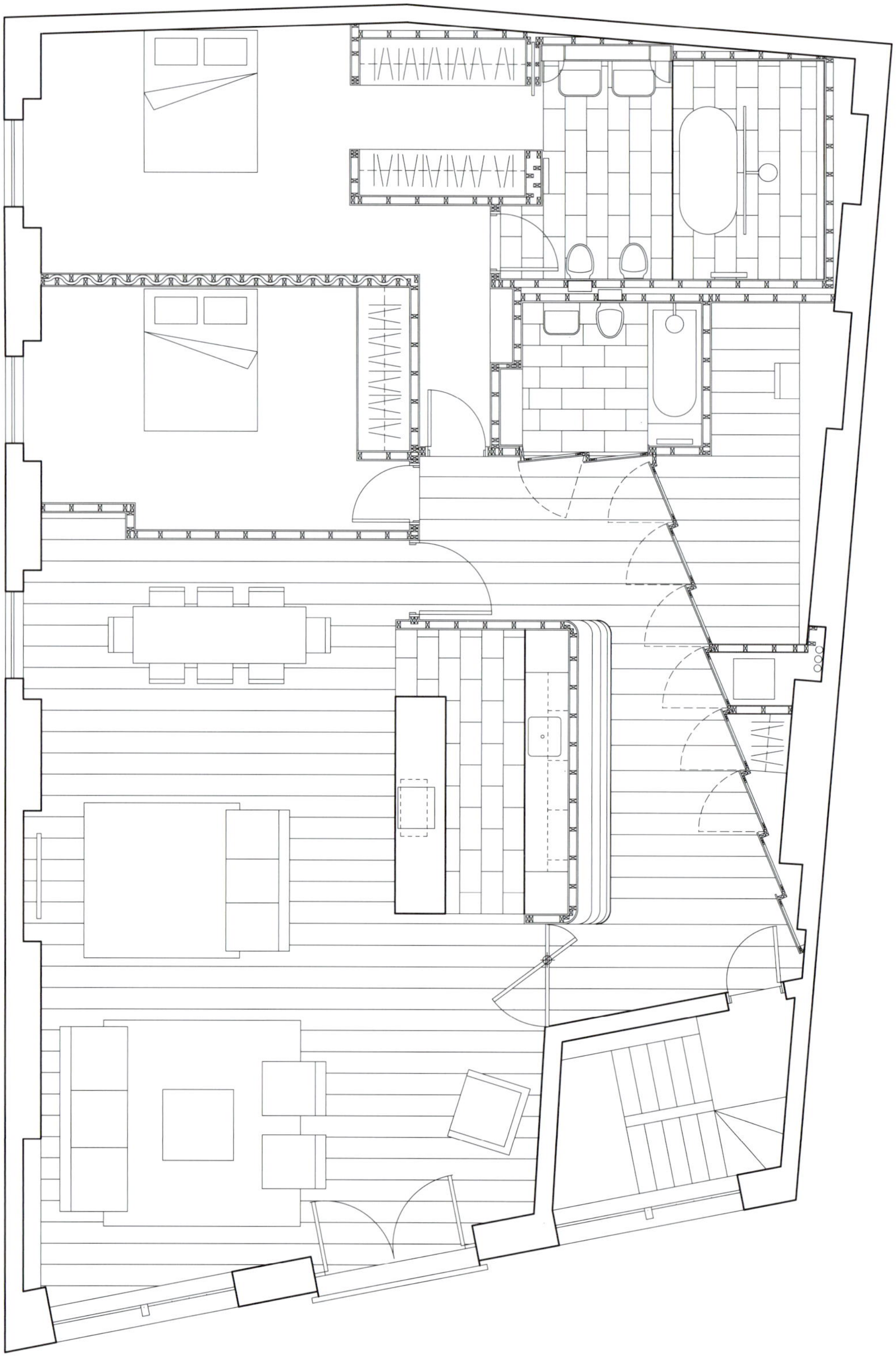

Above, Hall, with stepped doors open.
Middle, Kitchen.
Bottom, Hall bathroom.

Private Client, London, UK
Canyon Apartment
loft renovation, 2012

Canyon, a remodelling of an existing warehouse in Southwark, London uses a central kitchen pod to create multiple circulations in this flat. This sloped, felt covered pod which reads as a large object, and an opposite wall of eight stepped facet doors create an animated space unlike a typical hallway. The tilt back of the pod surface and the diagonal wall of doors create a canyon circulation with widest area leading to the pivoting 1500 mm living room door and the narrow end leading to the bedrooms. The pod was wrapped in 8 mm industrial felt working as an effective sound insulator for an entry space. The stepped doors provide handholds which invite opening into storage, washing, and office areas.

The social space opens to the left through the wide pivoting door. A 1.5 m wide pivoting door was designed to create a dramatic entrance to the living room and dining area and relate to existing loft facade doors.

Tupi Chairs

cafe, dining, and lounge chairs, 2014

Tupi is a collection of stackable chairs exploring the potential of hand weaving by mixing different coloured strips woven onto **a continous** curvelinear structure. The design explores weaving processes from two different cultures: traditional european cane cafe chairs and native Brazilian artefacts. Woven cane chairs became popular in the last century in Southern Brazil. These chairs are woven on a flat structure or surface with a consistent material usually natural cane. Procter-Rihl explores this technique further on a continuous flowing frame which generates a new tensioned curving surface. By weaving different colours, a typical solution done by native Brazilian tribes such as the Tupi tribes in Southern Brazil, the pattern distortions are emphasised.

The chair was designed with a very low back support to allow different positions for the user and fit snuggly under a table. The flipped folded down back functions as a handle for this very lightweight chair. Armrests on some chairs are continuation of the rear legs.

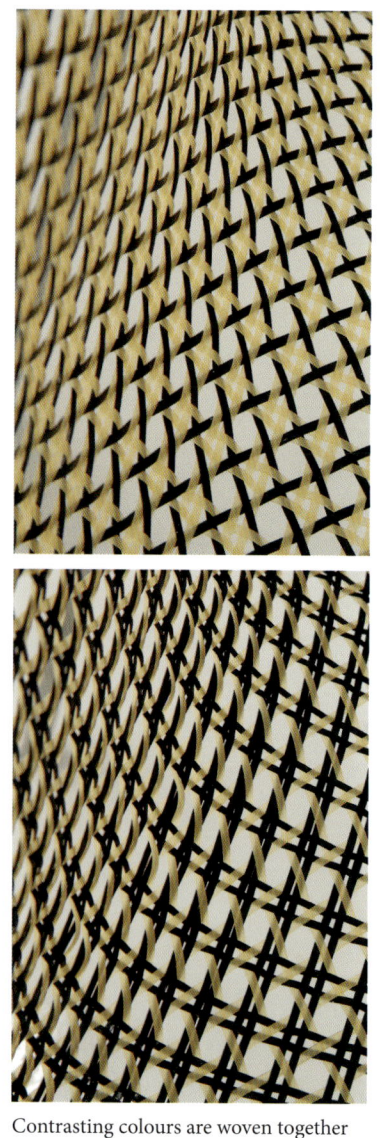

Contrasting colours are woven together to emphasise the distortions in the weave.

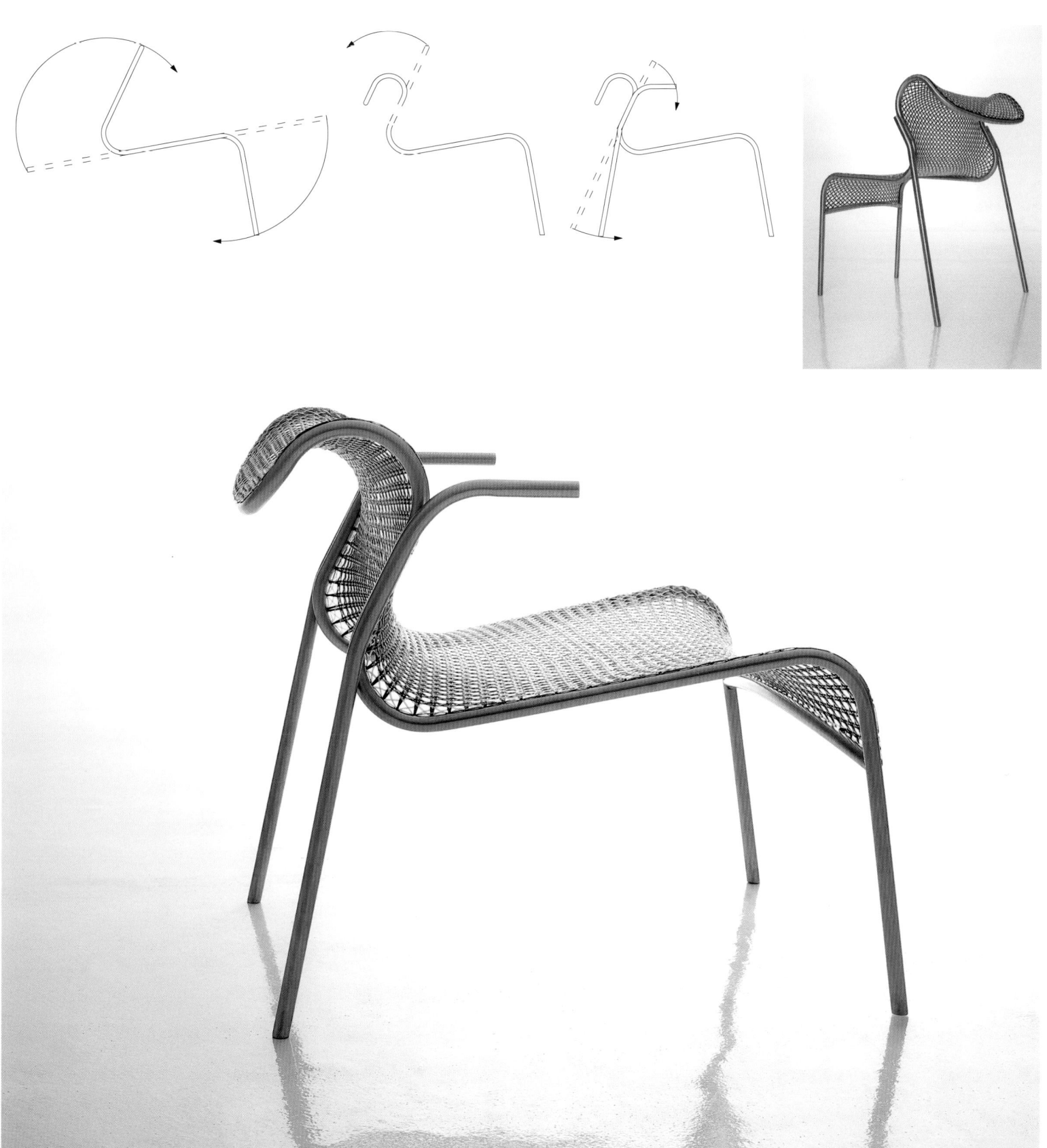

Private Client, London, UK
Scoop Extension
extension to victorian house, 2012

Scoop aims to maximise daylight in a rear extension to a typical Victorian terrace house in London. The brief was to design a highly energy efficient structure employing modern methods of construction. Rather than the recent spate of conservation approved glass boxes on existing structures, the project favours a more sustainable addition with thick insulted walls and ceiling. Daylight from the south facing clerestory window is reflected off the top kitchen cabinets to the ceiling in summer and directly through this window in winter. This clerestory is essentially a light scoop window above the existing garden wall. The roof is folded to fit under existing rear windows and angle up to the south to maximise winter solar gains. The extension follows Passivhaus principles with thick insulted walls and roof, compact plan and studied window orientation. The walls and roof are both made of 200 mm SIPS (Structural Insulating Panel) technology with a simliar 200 mm foam underfloor insulation, which gave maximum thermal and structural performance without cold bridges.

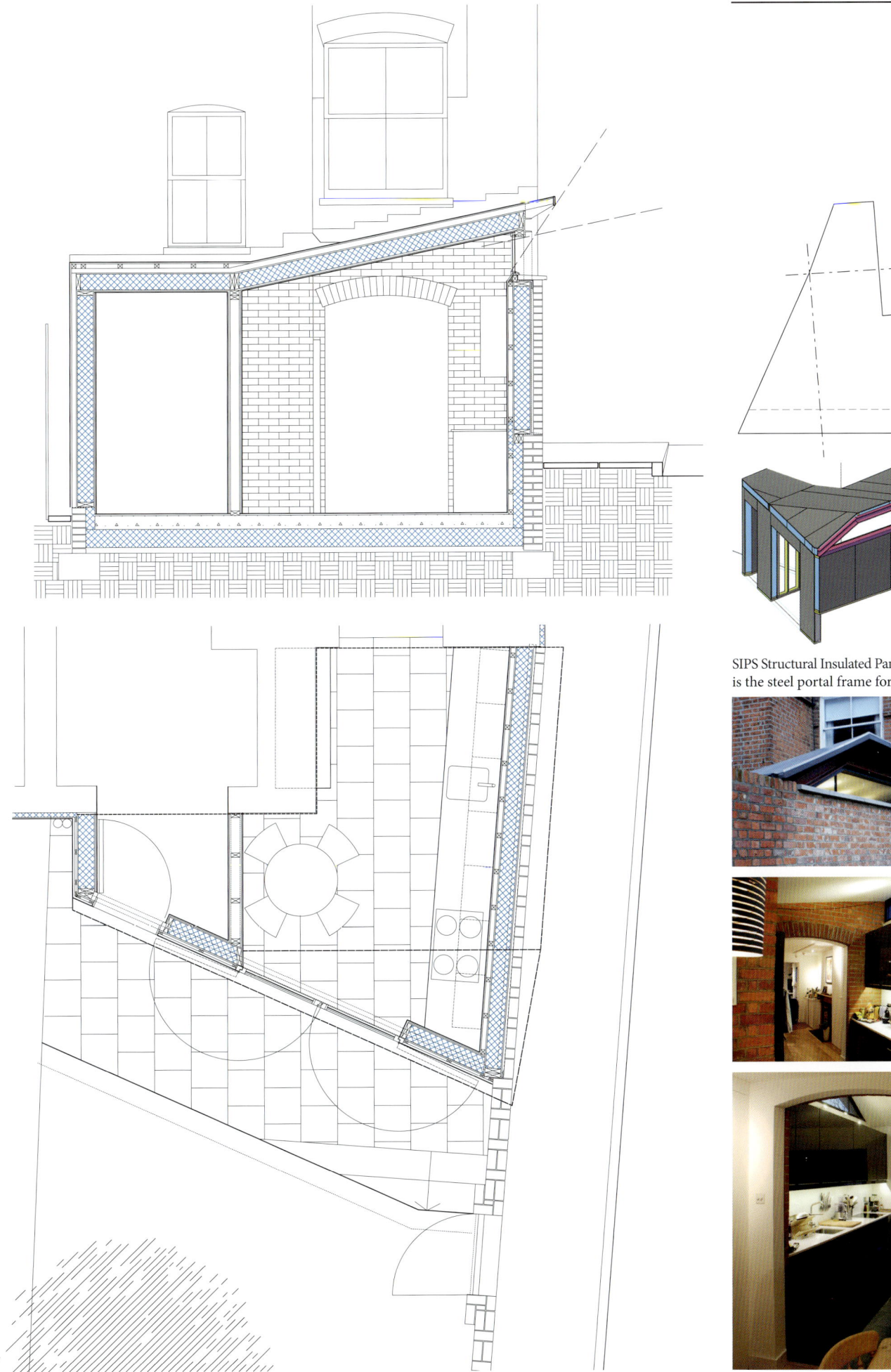

SIPS Structural Insulated Panels layout. Pink is the steel portal frame for the window.

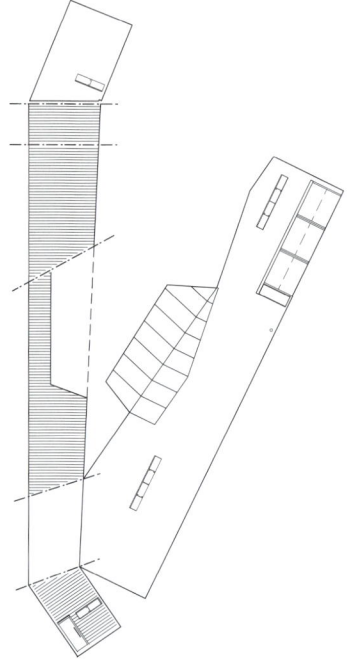

Right, view from master bedroom looking into the internal courtyard. The grills have a triple purpose of privacy, security, and filtering light. The grill becomes visually permeable depending on the viewing point.

Middle, the pet cat has his own private entrance through the concrete side wall.

Below, image of the narrow site and pubic pavement before construction.

<u>Private Client, Porto Alegre, Brazil</u>

Slice House

<u>new urban house, 2005</u>

Slice House explores the concept of a typical colonial Brazilian urban house and its flat facade, limited number of openings and a recessed folded roof. The house is placed on a 3.7 m wide x 38.5 m long site, resulting from the opening of a street 25 years ago. Residual sites are extremely interesting as they impose difficult questions to solve in terms of planning and programming. The non-orthogonal nature of the site, as it flares out a metre wider to 4.85 m at the rear, suggested to us we could use perspective to advantage to amplify the space.

    The client followed our advice to purchase the site when it went on auction for a fifth time. Schematically the house is divided in two sections by a large outdoor courtyard. The courtyard balances daylight in such a long site giving, as well as providing, privacy to the main bedroom at the rear above the garage. A very small palette of materials was used to balance some complex geometries (corrugated metal roofing, wood plank formed concrete and white plaster).

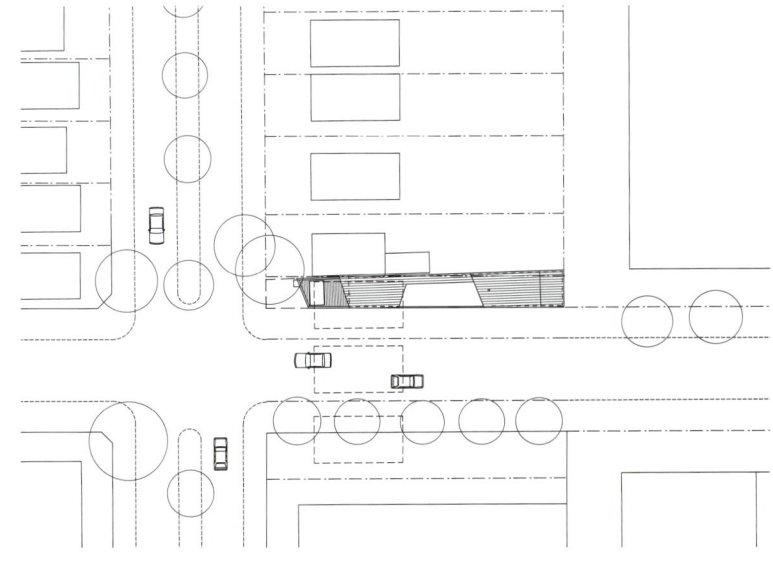

Swimming and Other Domestic Practices

The design of the pool illustrates the cult of the body and voyeurism in Brazilian society. The pool polarises the attention in the house mixing voyeurism with other domestic practices, not normally associated with nudity, such as cooking and eating. The private swimming pool has always become closely associated with modernism since last century. Adolf Loos designed a house for Josephine Baker in the late 1920s with a swimming pool at street level turning the actress' exhibitionist behaviour into performance art.

A sense of immersion is achieved by a precise control of daylight in the space. At different times of the day, sunlight pierces through the swimming pool creating a series of rippling effects on walls and ceilings. Daylight becomes soft and gentle balanced by other 4 m long slot window in the space creating a dream-like quality of the moving water during the day. At night, with the pool lights on, it works as a large coloured light fitting where a blue light washes the space.

Right, pool terrace view out from the guest bedroom defines a non-orthogonal space. It gives a sense of privacy but also frames a 50-year-old Flamboyant tree.

Above, the floating tank above the living area suggests a sense of immersion with the sky seen through the water.

The tilted ceiling rises from the master bedroom as one approaches the living room.

Mirrors suggest an expansion of space in the master bathroom.

The concrete ceiling folds down on a 12 degree slope towards the bedroom.

Complex Geometrics and Spatial Illusions

The studio decided to emphasise linearity instead of neutralising it on this narrow site. A series of angled cross-walls or tilted horizontal ceilings fold within the form generating strong spatial illusions. Never perpendicular, the longer length cross-walls give the appearance of a wider space. As users try to decode complex geometries, space becomes richer as the brain projects orthogonally. Visual perception tends to tunnel in, making space appear to be smaller. As the site is non-orthogonal increasing in width from 3.7 to 4.8 m this natural perspective is neutralised. This condition from the living room creates the illusion of a bigger space. Most of the ground floor is a continuous open social space with an internal courtyard giving unexpected depth to this domestic environment.

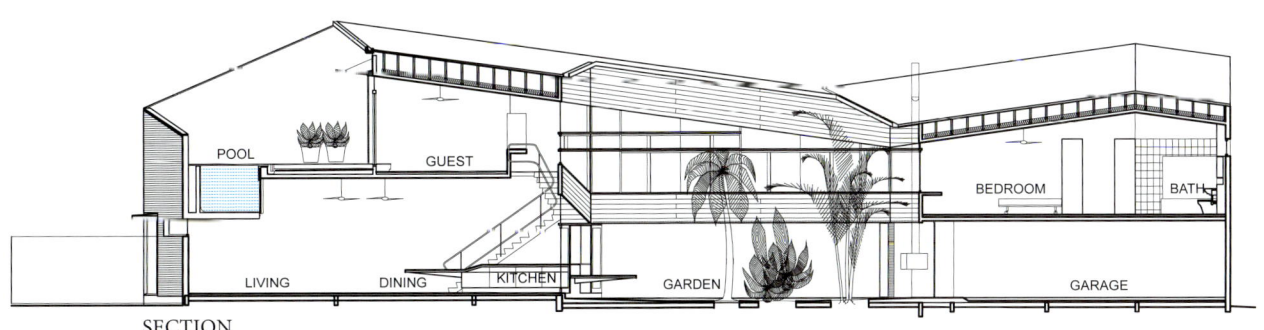

SECTION

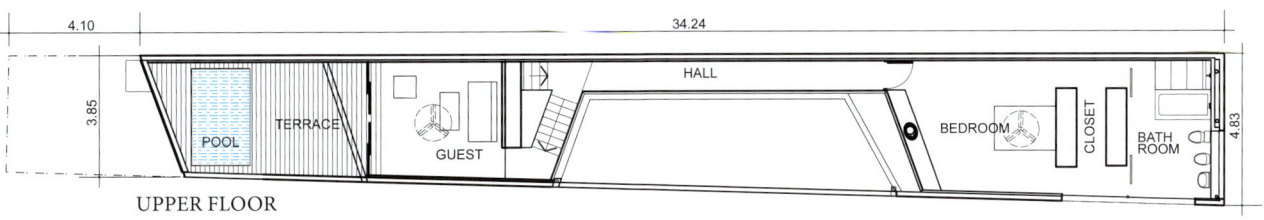

4.10

3.85

34.24

4.83

UPPER FLOOR

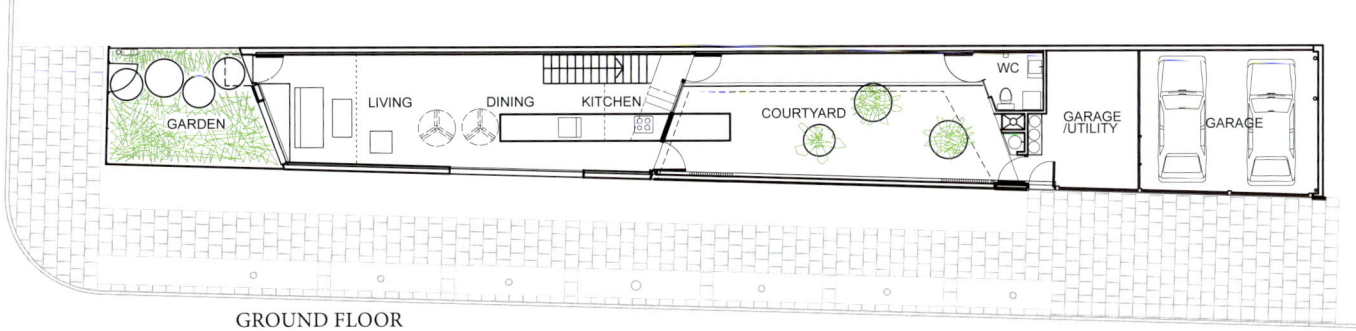

GROUND FLOOR

M

Right, the upper storey connecting corridor between the guest and master bedrooms. Height is accentuated by a 10 degree concrete sloping slab. The exposed concrete was formed with wood planks which follow the angled beam stair wall.

Below, the other side of this hall envelope closes in towards the private zones reaching its lowest height of 2.1 m at the master bedroom door.

The Familiar and The Extraordinary

The familiar is explored by historical residential typology and materiality. The project follows a typical colonial Brazilian urban house typology usually called "sobrado" with its flat facade, folded roof, limited number of openings, and blank side walls and courtyard. Everyday materials were used in the project such as the corrugated metal and wood plank formed concrete.

The extraordinary comes into play through an exploration of complex geometries. The house is conceived as a prismatic volume. Materials follow the continuity of planes such as the metallic roof as it folds onto the facade plane. The surface is completed by an industrial grill system completely covering the courtyard with the purpose of filtering daylight and creating security for the occupants. They can walk freely in the space without worrying about security or privacy as the heavier vertical fins also create privacy for the users as they block views from outside. At night, these fins reflect internal lighting creating a shimmering effect.

This transparency of the grills is also shown in the fence of the front entry garden. From a direct forward view the grill disappears and the continous planting through the fence is clearly visible. From an angled view the fence obsures the view as seen on page 53.

The living room viewed from the front entry under the pool.

The grills on the courtyard roof complete the prismatic geometry with an ethereal quality duc to its permeability.

Left, narrow front entry garden facade. The three key materials used are corrugated metal roofing, white plaster interior surfaces and expressive wood plank-formed concrete.

Brazilian Picturesque: Informal Planting

The concept was to offset the prismatic geometry of the house with a wild natural aesthetic. Most of the plants specified in the internal and external gardens were native plants. Colours employed are hues of purples and whites with a few orange clashes. Three different zones were identified: entrance garden (partially sunny/damp), side garden wall strip (sunny/dry/windy) and internal courtyard (filtered light/protected). The front entry garden was planted in layered heights and different foliage scales around an offset path of concrete circles. Four planting drifts flow through the fence into the side garden: the aubergine brown phormium tenax spikes purple iris flowers on green spikes noemarica caerulea, and in front the low growing white grass lirope muscari around clumps of orange bird of paradise strelitzia juncea thin stalks. The side garden against the concrete wall following the principles of an English border garden of mixed and layered plant height groupings. Various types of spiky agave and aloe vera protect corners with tall yucca, *Dracaena marginata*, and *Durenta repens* against the wall. In the courtyard, palms and banana species were planted in three large submerged concrete pipes to create the effect of a tropical forest with hammocks strung from wall to wall.

Different types of Bromelias were planted in the entrance garden.

Different types of Agaves colonised the side garden.

Round stepping pads are played as voids in the internal garden.

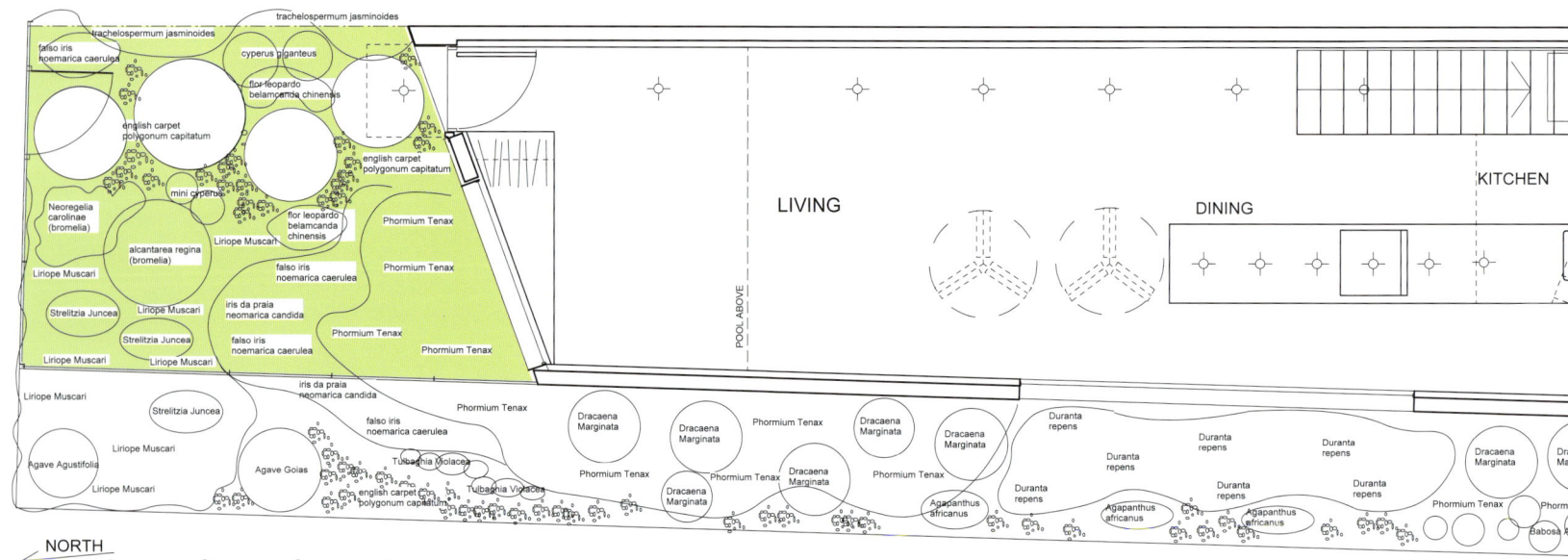

Planting drifts through the grill to the side garden.

Hammocks in the courtyard.

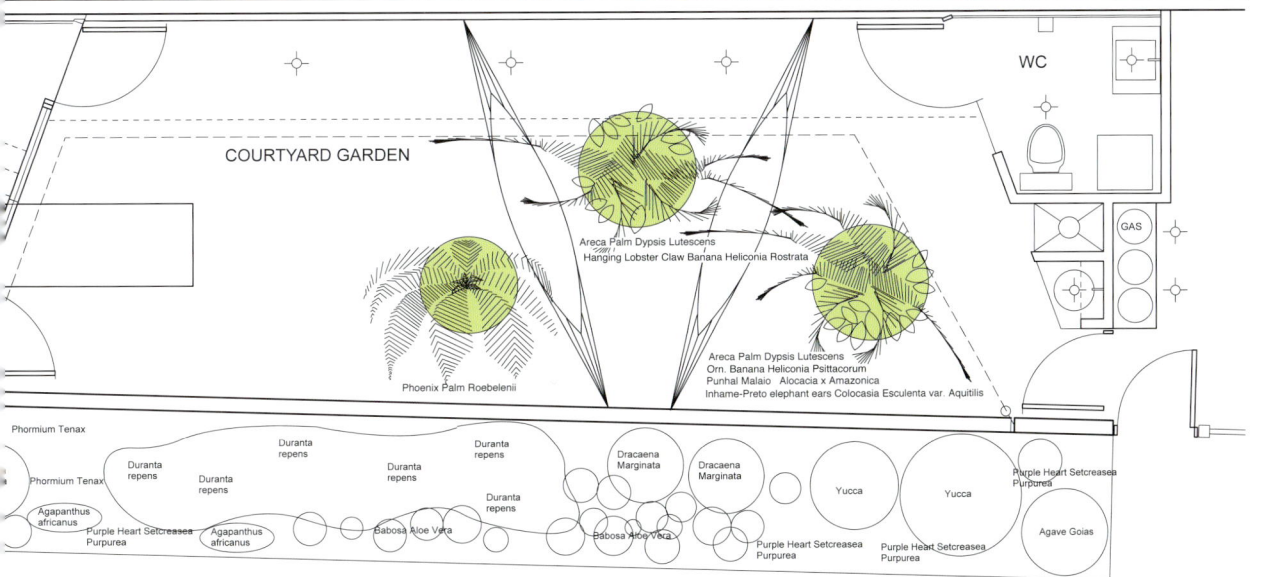

COURTYARD GARDEN

WC

GAS

Areca Palm Dypsis Lutescens
Hanging Lobster Claw Banana Heliconia Rostrata

Phoenix Palm Roebelenii

Areca Palm Dypsis Lutescens
Orn. Banana Heliconia Psittacorum
Punhal Malaio Alocacia x Amazonica
Inhame-Preto elephant ears Colocasia Esculenta var. Aquitilis

Phormium Tenax

Phormium Tenax

Duranta
repens

Duranta
repens

Duranta
repens

Duranta
repens

Duranta
repens

Duranta
repens

Dracaena
Marginata

Dracaena
Marginata

Yucca

Yucca

Purple Heart Setcreasea
Purpurea

Agapanthus
africanus

Purple Heart Setcreasea
Purpurea

Agapanthus
africanus

Babosa Aloe Vera

Babosa Aloe Vera

Purple Heart Setcreasea
Purpurea

Purple Heart Setcreasea
Purpurea

Agave Goias

Top, the continous loop stair balustrade.

Above, 8 mm steel plate accordion stair underneath which the purple kitchen storage block.

Furniture as Space Generators

The pool, the staircase, and the dining/kitchen counter were key elements used to generate space in this house. They define zones for different domestic practices in this large living space. The suspended pool forms a lower ceiling over the living room seating and doubles as a window or spectacle. At different times of the day, daylight enters the social area creating a shimmering effect on walls and ceiling. At night, the pool becomes a key light fitting as artifical light bounces on its planes creating a sense of immersion to the space.

The dining kitchen counter cantilevers 2.2 m on both sides creating lightness to this heavy steel piece of furniture. Food is laid out on both wings of the object for either internal or outdoor meals. A double-sided kitchen basin transitions the different height between kitchen preparation and lower table height eating. The counter is finished with a high gloss polyurethane, a non-scratch paint usually used in labs and in the airplane industry. The 7 m counter reinforces the linear condition of the site and allows free circulation through doors on both sides to the courtyard beyond.

The stair is a 8 mm steel plate accordion, which wraps around and above the kitchen counter. Its thin edge is emphasised in light grey contrasted with the exposed underside painted in a deep aubergine purple. The thin 32 mm upright tubes support and 35 mm handrail, which forms a looped continuous top handrail and lower thigh height bottom rail. The balustrade leans out with the handrail atop the upright and an ankle height rail pulled in giving a sensation of safety to a fairly open balustrade.

All furniture was commissioned; including bed, chairs, arm chairs and the usual in-built furniture, as well as the mail box. There is a special circular hole in the concrete courtyard wall for a cat entry.

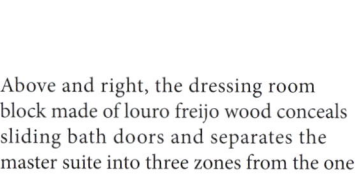

Above and right, the dressing room block made of louro freijo wood conceals sliding bath doors and separates the master suite into three zones from the one grand space. Customised bed and chair.

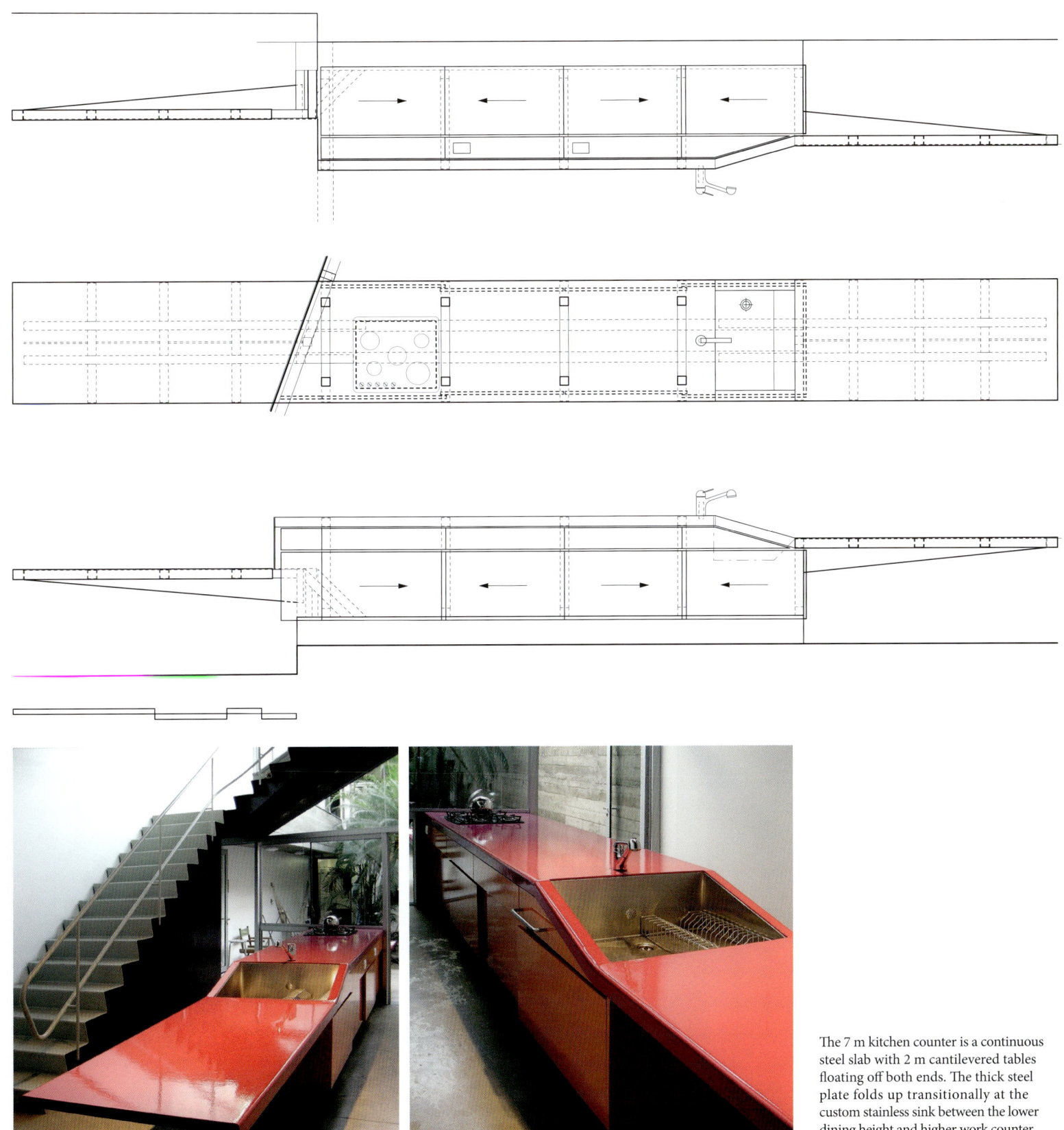

The 7 m kitchen counter is a continuous steel slab with 2 m cantilevered tables floating off both ends. The thick steel plate folds up transitionally at the custom stainless sink between the lower dining height and higher work counter. The counter was coated with hard polyurethane, a high gloss non-scratch paint usually used in labs.

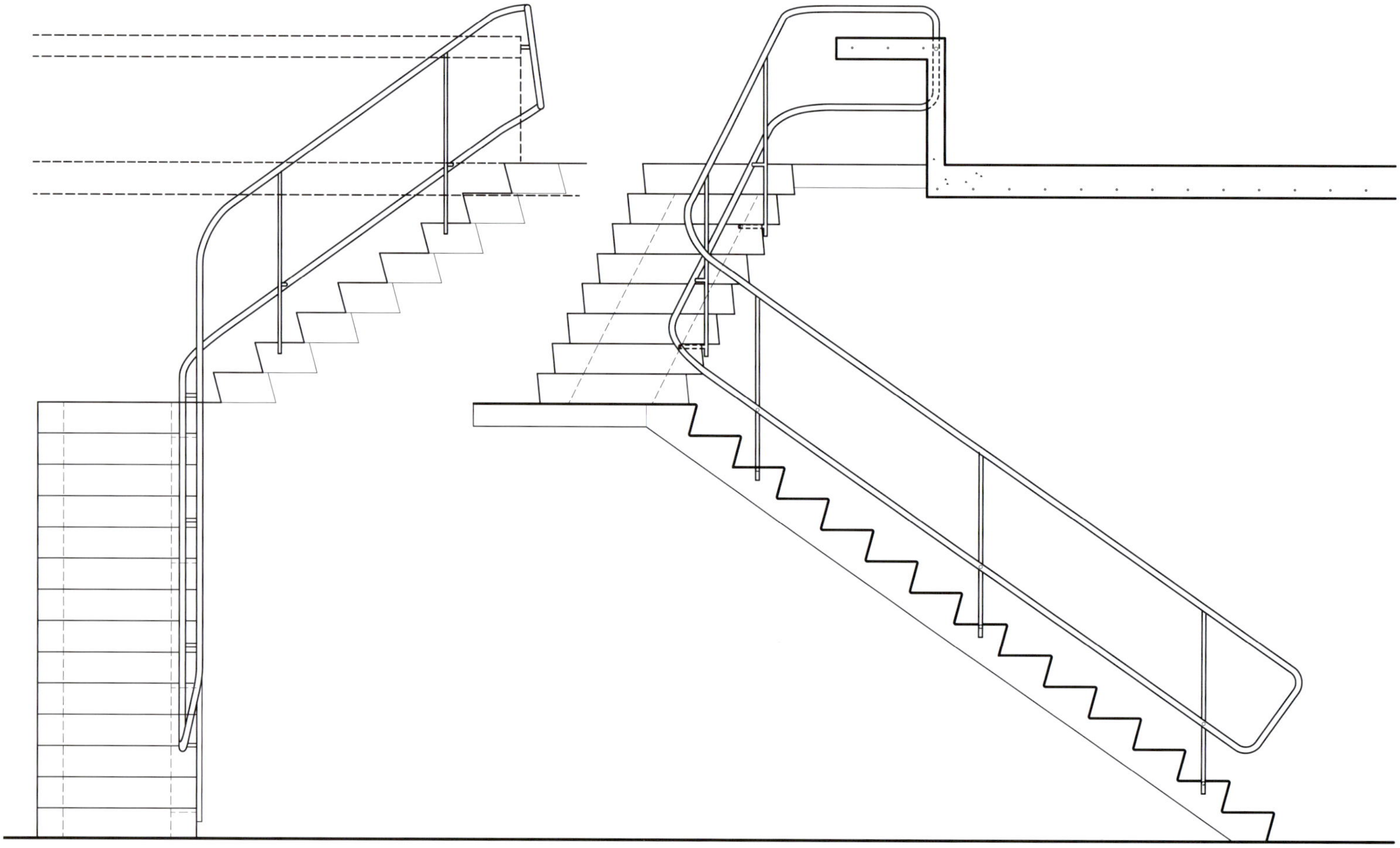

The handrail is a continous loop with the lowest bar set in and the upper rail aligned to
the stair edge. Strength is given from the U-shape bracing which allows fine member sizes.
The stair and pool were engineered in the UK while the concrete was engineered in Brazil.

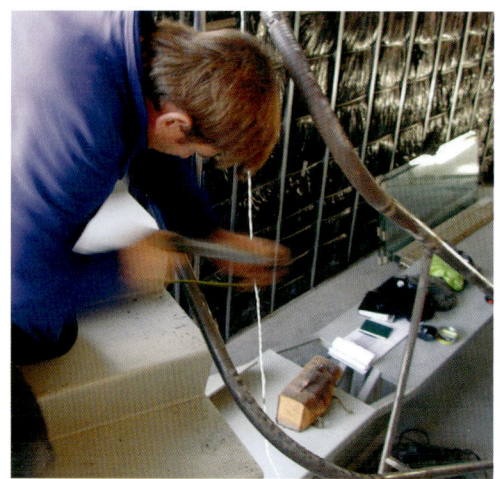

The swimming pool resin coat on concrete, looking from the living room below.

The pool and terrace roof were clad with the same material.

Steel dining cantilever structure in the courtyard.

The small gap allowing rain to flow down this plane.

Lifting the upper steel stair into place.

Welding the handrail on site.

Peabody Housing Trust, Palmers Garage, London
Pinch Housing
eight unit housing competition, 2014

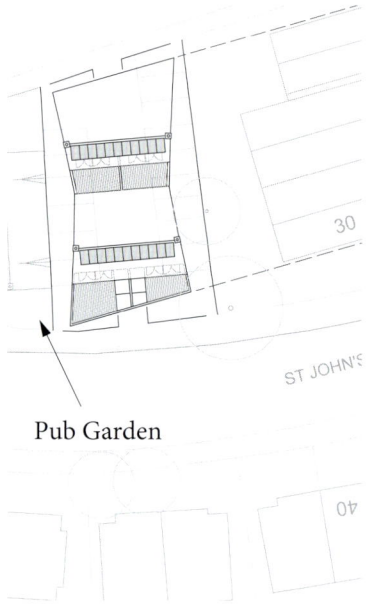

Pub Garden

Pinch makes a series of vernacular references to British residential architecture through its design language and materiality. Its folded geometry is a reflection of its immediate context as the building becomes a connecting piece between the adjacent non-aligned buildings. Folding happens vertically down the pinched sides and undulates across the roofs and street facades clad with roofing tiles. The building centre has been pinched in to provide more light and wider outdoor space back from the street. Key local materials such as red brick and slate roofing also reflect the industrial heritage of victorian London.

The design was a competition entry for a housing scheme for the Peabody Housing Trust in London. This multiple housing complex follows Passivhaus principles with thick insulted walls and roof, compact plan, and windows oriented for solar gain. All eight flats have outdoor spaces of either gardens or roof terraces. Top flats have an inverted social layout directly connected to outside sky terraces for the four maisonettes. The building is designed with no communal circulation. Its eight independant private entries reduce maintenance and security issues and create a sense of ownership. The ground floor flats were designed as disabled friendly environments (orange circles are wheelchair turning circles).

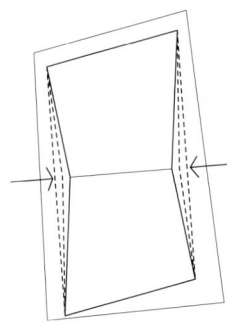

The building was pinched to allow more daylight into the centre of the structure — space for existing trees and yards.

GROUND FLOOR

FIRST FLOOR

SECOND FLOOR

N

Solar Collectors

Summer 21 June

Winter 21 Dec

Blue is one-bed accessible flat with outdoor yard.

Orange is two-bed maisonette with sky terrace.

Perforate

Investigating Skins, Surfaces and Planes

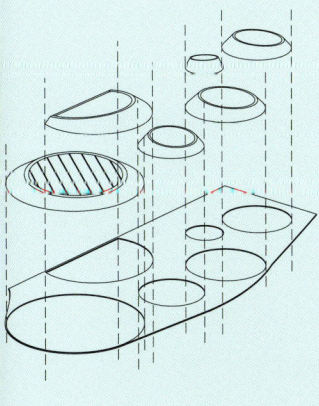

Perforate rekindles our interest in skins, surfaces and planes. All projects grouped in this section have in common a continuous surface that has been cut through either by cutting, tearing, splitting, rupturing or dividing. It is a surface intervention that inevitably leads to bold formal results as the action inevitably suggests an element of destruction.

Perforate, at first glance, has a very precise meaning that suggests a circular puncture on a thin material but it can also be defined as "to enter" or "to extend through". The studio explores this action as a rupture on a surface that is not necessarily round, that can be multiplied, cut, or split, leading to tearing.

The action has a revealing quality of expressing another world or space as the "perforation" is destructive and revealing at the same time. It can also give depth to a fairly thin surface as it can be multiplied across several surfaces creating a deep tri-dimensional object. Perforate is usually developed with complementary actions such as extend, extrude or twist.

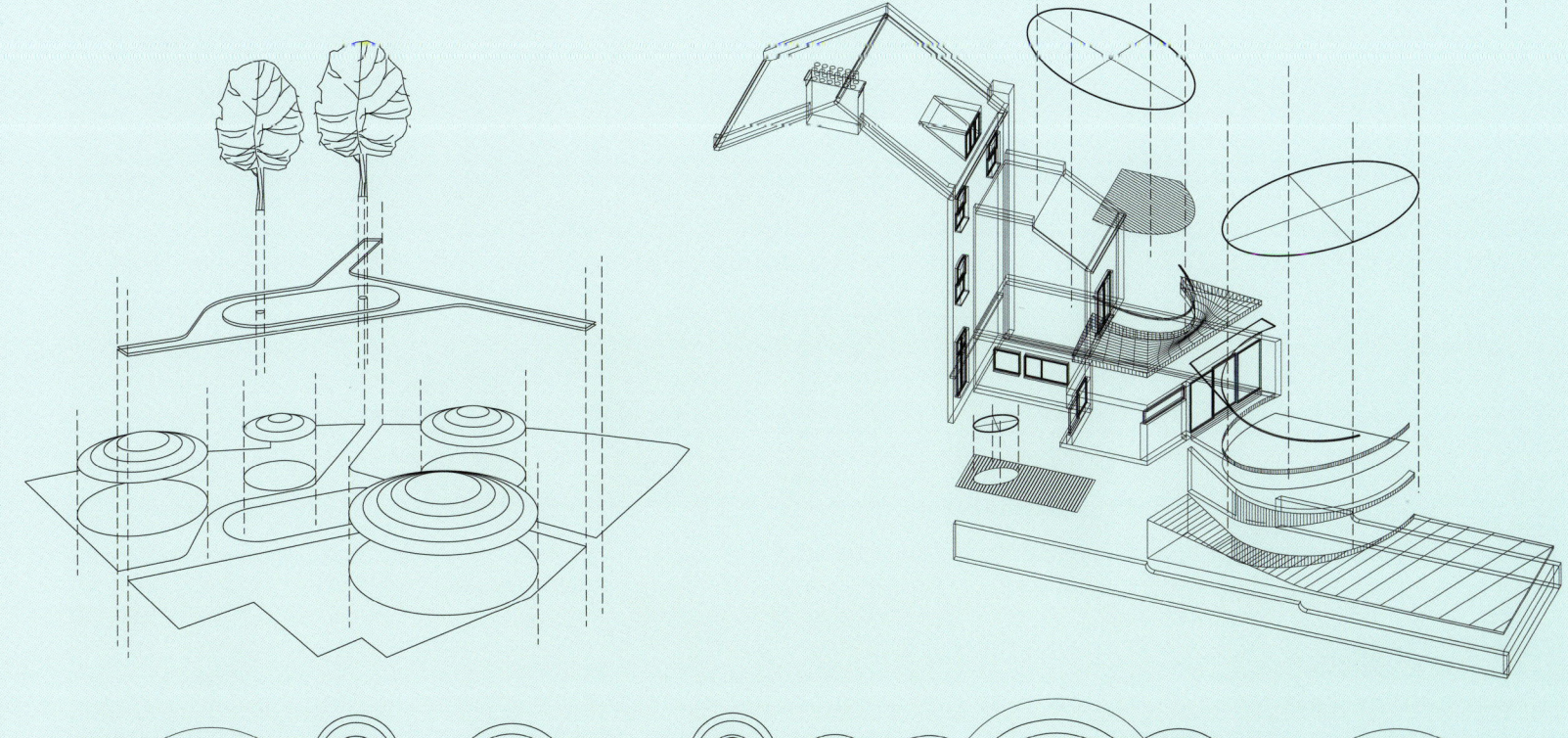

Cocada Preta, Brazil
As Coxudas
in development, 2014-2016

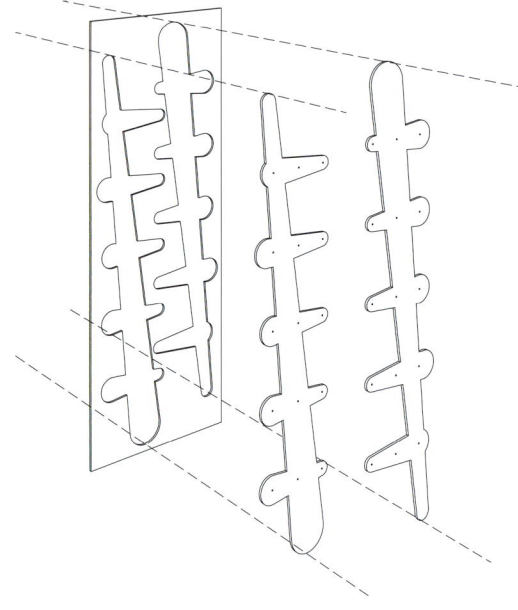

As Coxudas line explores mass through the manipulation of planes or surfaces. The design tests anthropomorphic shapes in furniture, (as coxudas is Brazilian slang for thick thighs). The pieces have dual aesthetics that look voluptous from some views but skinny from others.

The material is a coated MDF with the cut edge exposing the inner MDF material. This creates an outline to the piece which expresses its production as punched from sheet material. The small storage system was designed as an object that leans agaisnt the wall. The table tops are fixed with invisible pegs suggesting these planes are floating on legs. The furniture line was designed for efficient production with a minimum amount of components and fixings. All pieces are interlocking pieces cut by CNC technology and are flat packed.

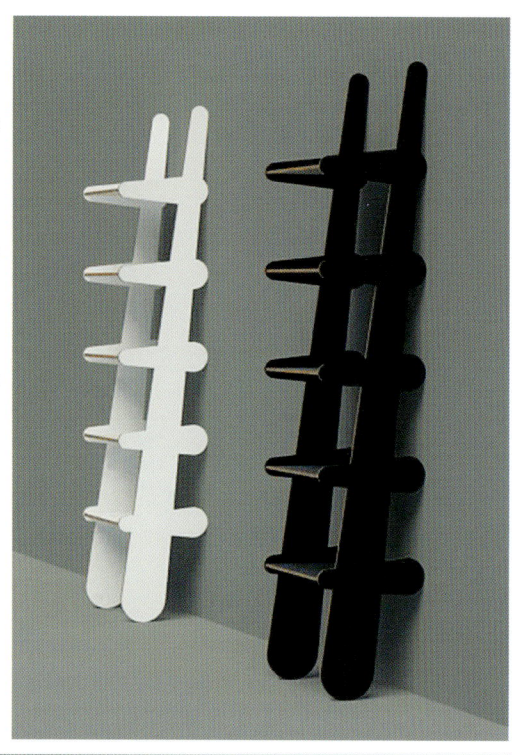

As Coxudas plays with a very flat aesthetic using 2-D planes.

Procter-Rihl, London, UK
Ozone Table
limited edition, 1995–1999

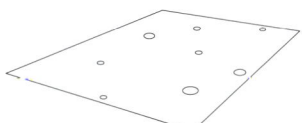 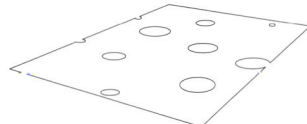 

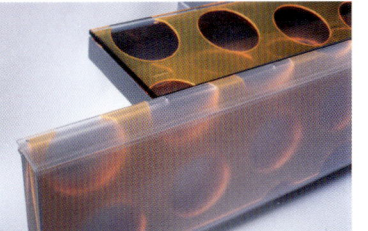

Ozone explores a sense of weightlessness. A single piece of acrylic was layered between two sheets of glass to create perforated surface voids playing with perception, allowing views through to magazines on the glass shelf below or floating coffee cups. In 1995 it was the first furniture to use flourescent live-edge acrylic, a material which intensifies light at any cut polished edge. Originally designed for the Bento Box penthouse on page 88 it was launched at the first 100% Design, London.

It was produced in a limited edition of 50 between 1995–1999. Four prototypes were shown with a T section steel frame 600 x 900 x 35 mm then in 1996 it was launched in a L angle frame 700 x 945 x 34 mm in seven colours; opal, frost white, live-edge orange, live-edge blue, live-edge green, glass green, and a one-off transparent pink for the Colette shop, Paris. A frost white piece was made in 1999 for the new British Embassy in Moscow. In 1997 a reception desk for the British Council, Singapore used the live-edge orange circles arranged into the Council's x logo, angled behind a glass top and frosted front panel (right).

Private Client, London, UK
Liquid Sky Apartment
loft apartment renovation, 2014

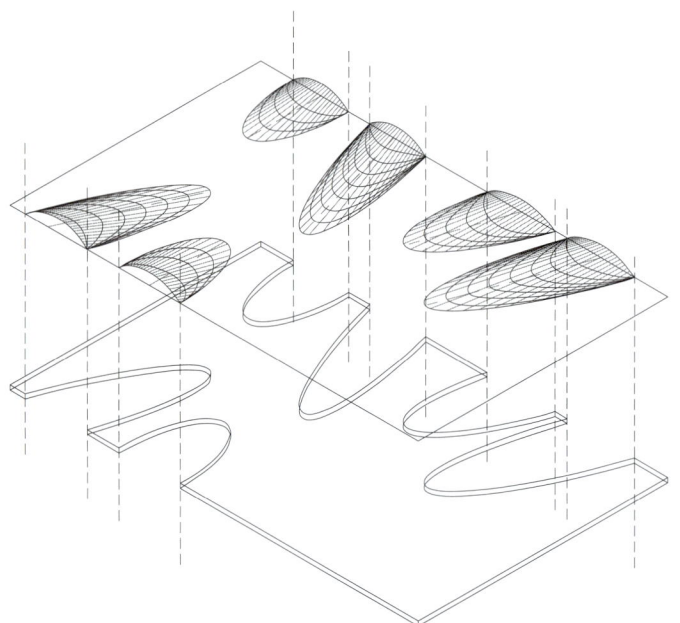

Liquid Sky explores topographic contours cut into an existing ceiling. There was an awkward ceiling, which dropped below the original window height that was clumsily added by the developer, for soundproof reasons, when the flats were subdivided. The opportunity to correct this led us to a series of oval perforations carved up to the top of the windows. The elliptical geometry was defined by the mapping of sun paths into the space. As the sun moves into the space it fills the scoops with light creating a sculptural ceiling surface. All artificial lighting was designed to be from below by floor lamps keeping the ceiling an intact continuous surface without interuptions. The light scoops were originally going to be fabricated using CNC technology but they were built *in situ* for a fraction of the price.

The commission also consisted of a complete remodelling with new kitchen and the addition of a WC and two ensuite bathrooms. The kitchen was rotated 90 degrees in the space with access at both ends to generate easy and fluid circulation. All edges were smooth to create continuous fluid surfaces.

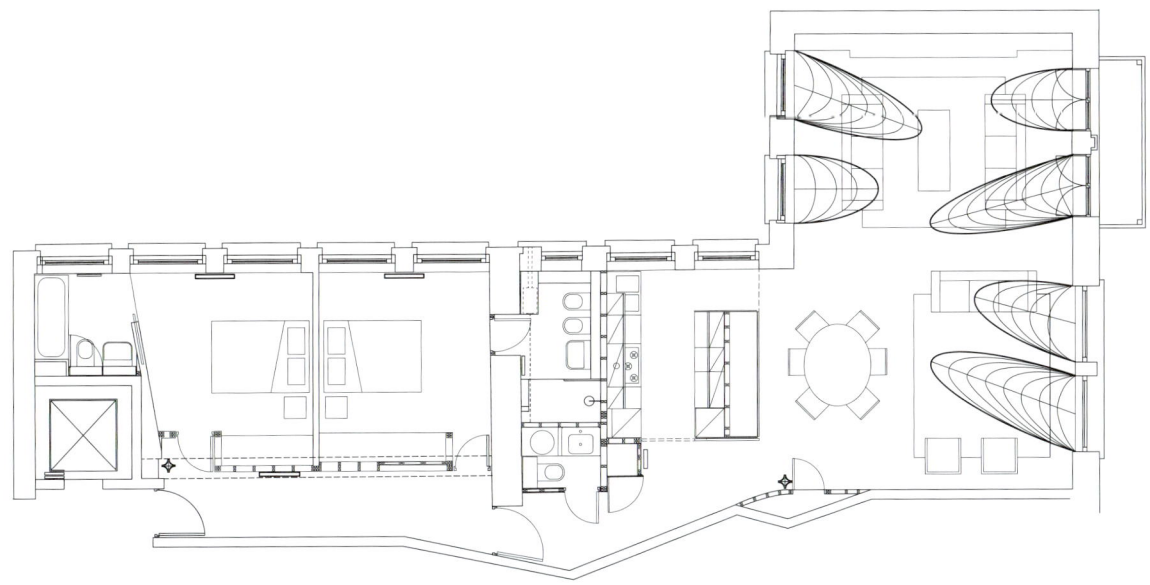

Plan showing ceiling perforations in the living room.

White Carrara kitchen reflects on the bronze splashback extending visually the counter space. Ensuite bathroom was clad with Badiglio marble and master bathroom in Carrara marble.

Extension with garden sweeping up to the green roof.

Custom-made triple sliding doors create openess towards the garden with a high level slot window for neighbours privacy.

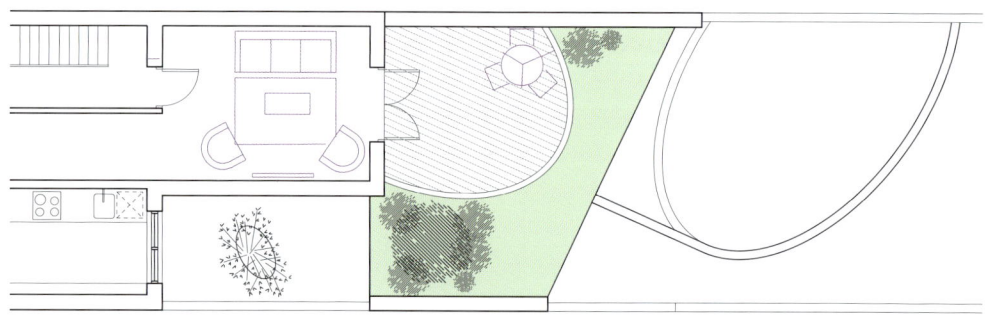

First (upper) floor flat with ellipse deck on the roof terrace garden.

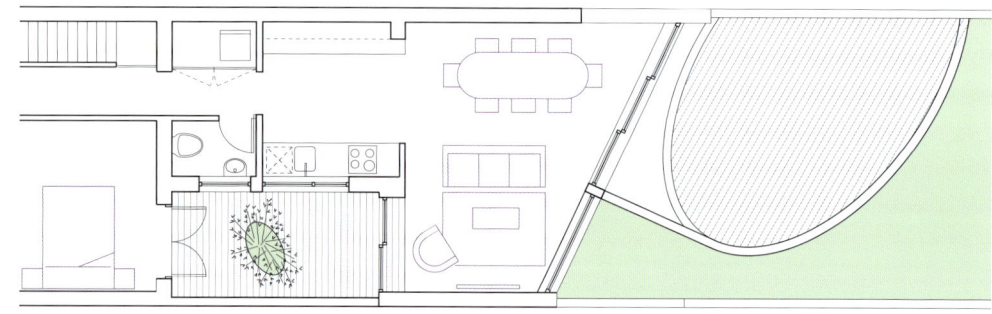

Ground floor flat with the bamboo ellipse handrail (below) on the courtyard deck with the ellipse deck in the rear garden (above).

Private Clients, London, UK
Three Ellipses Extension
house extension/ landscape, 2001

Three Ellipses explores contouring of the garden topography for a new rear extension. The ground landscape was lifted diagonally up towards the roof to create the illusion of a continous surface. A planted green roof was created extending the garden up onto this higher level. Most green roofs are planted with sedum and shallow soil and thus do not allow a variety of plant sizes. This roof has an artificial slope made of stacked layers of foam insulation creating an insulated structure and deeper pockets of soil higher up the roof to allow larger plants to grow.

The commission was from two clients with single floor apartments in this divided London terrace house. This design gave each apartment a garden; the ground floor the rear garden and the upper floor the planted roof terrace. Three ellipses perforate three social zones: garden terrace, upper deck, and the internal courtyard. The design maximises daylight and solar penetration by tilting the facade towards the south. Triple sliding doors allow the dining area to be easily connected to outdoors and a deep shading device was designed to protect from summer radiation. The ground floor flat was completely remodelled adding an extra bedroom with the new configuration.

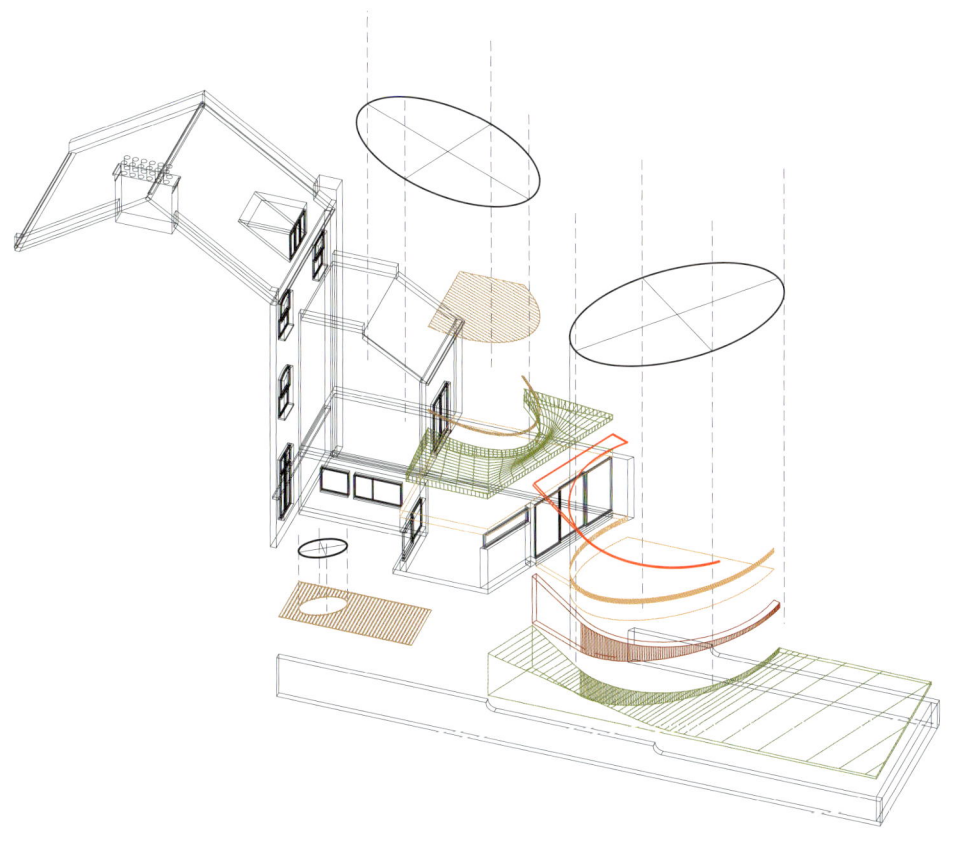

The green barrier towards the neighbour was a strategic idea to respond to privacy concerns from adjacent neighbours. At the edge of the roof sedum was planted to create a slim roof edge. The photo, left previous page, shows a permanent cafe table made of stainless steel with frosted acrylic top, designed as part of the balustrade.

Cocada Preta , Brazil
Strata, Prion Tables and Boxes
limited editions, 1996 and 2016

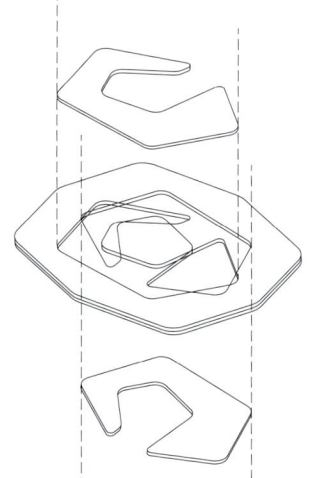

Strata explores the concepts of layering and transparency **with a digital sensibility. Inspired by the Brazilian landscape architect Roberto Burle Marx,** the organic shapes suggest biological organisms in petri dishes and microscopic slides. The use of live-edge acrylic brings a luminous edge observed in biology and a synthetic sensibility to the piece. Overlayered acrylic creates a third colour and suggests depth with different visual arrangements and permutations of acrylic types (matt, clear, translucent and live-edge). The cut form was flipped horizontally and vertically to simplify the manufacturing process as a single piece creating an optical illusion. The design led to innumerable one-offs either as permanent cladding systems, murals, screens, partitions or one-off furniture pieces. The 2016 edition below uses a tubular ss frame for greater transparency and weightlessness. **Prion boxes** 1996–1998 limited production of 100, were handmade, cut by jig, edge polished and heat folded in a North London workshop and sold at design galleries in Paris, Singapore, New York, Copenhagen, Sydney, Tokyo and London.

Far left, Prion Tables, limited production in three sizes and two colour combinations. The Prion Tables with the Ozone Table (p 63) were Procter-Rihl's first furniture pieces in 1995. The Prions were replaced by the lighter weight Strata in 1996.

Middle, the 1996 Strata Table lead to a series of one-off pieces. A 6 m wall cladding was designed in 1998 (right) to emphasise verticality in the stairwell of a housing, Camden, London.

Opposite page, 2016 Strata re-edition employs SS rod legs to emphasise its weightlessness and to create stronger light effects. The continuos loop pierces through the arcylic planes to form carry handles.
edition: Limited Edition
size: 70 mm x 45 mm x 43 mm high
colour: 6 colour combinations

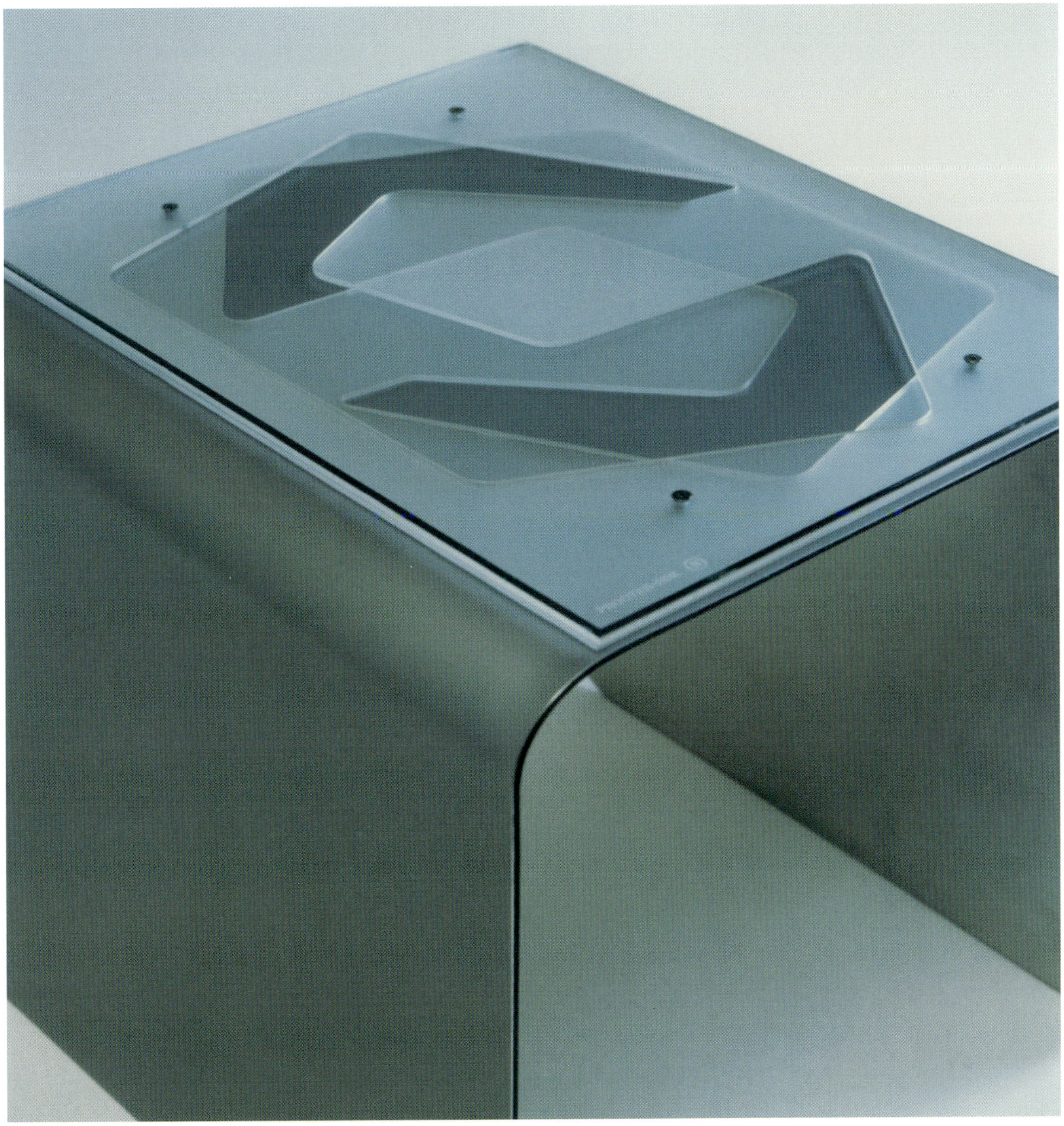

Left, the Strata was launched in 1996 and produced until 1998 on a limited production basis. The piece was made of an acylic, glass top with a lightweight thermoplastic aluminium base.
edition: Limited Edition of 50
size: 44 mm x 45 mm x 43 mm high
colour: 18 colour combinations

Below, the Prion Box 1996–1998 contemporary Japanese lacquer box.
edition: Limited Edition of 100
size: 25 mm x 19 mm x 8 mm high
colour: 17 colour combinations

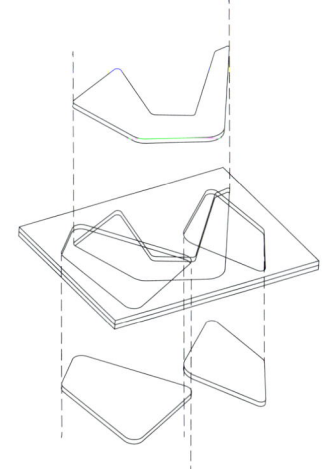

Nine Elms regeneration, London, UK
Pedestrian Rotary Gardens
public garden, 2015 to present

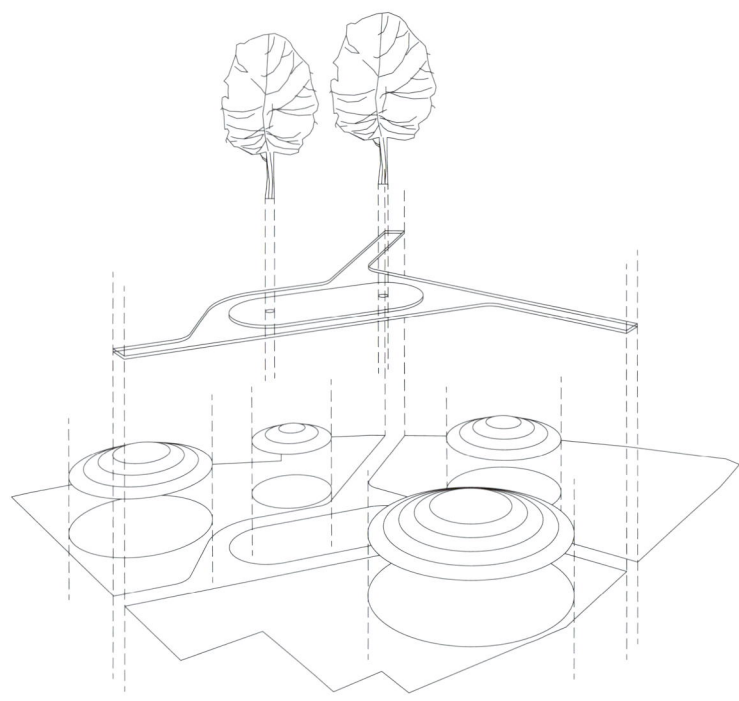

The pilot project Wild Meadow One was developed and built in 2015. In order to make the project sustainable, the studio set up a gardening club and several activities to engage residents. Below right, an image after three months of the meadow being seeded.

Pedestrian Rotary Gardens explores road traffic symbols in an extensive London public garden making a commentary on pace and movement in the city. The bold rotary symbols were played against a soft undulating meadow landscape with variable heights determined by mounds. The mounds have the purpose of creating privacy for the ground floor flats and a more interesting topography for the residents. The bold patterns were designed to be seen from above through windows and balconies in the four- to ten-storey residential blocks. The traffic symbols create several possibilities for different types of outdoor collective or private zones. The aim was to balance the natural and the artificial moving away from a romaticised view of the landscape where the natural blends with the artificial in a seamless manner.

The project was developed with local residents using participatory design methods in the design process. The design delivers a sustainable garden with a wild range of species and pollination to encourage wild life and bio diversity in the area. The design creates maximum ground permeability reducing the pressure on the existing Victorian sewage system in London. The studio believes in the need to design gardens more intelligently and more efficiently in terms of water management without the need for intensive maintenance. Future additions will be; allotment gardens, public furniture facilities such as seating, recycling facilities, bicycle parking, and a compost production area.

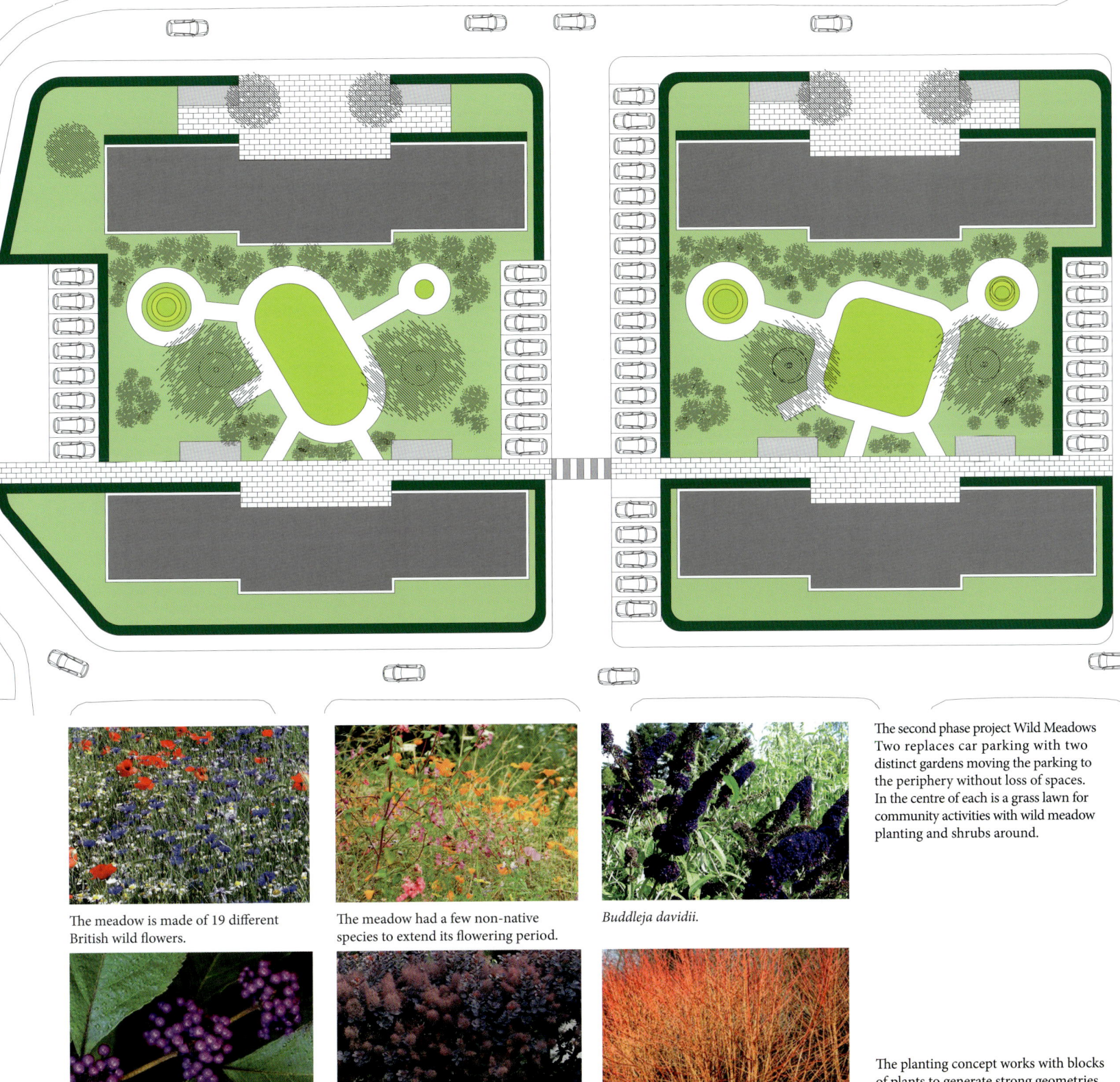

The meadow is made of 19 different British wild flowers.

The meadow had a few non-native species to extend its flowering period.

Buddleja davidii.

Callicarpa bodinieri.

Cotinus coggygria.

Cornus sanguinea — dogwood.

The second phase project Wild Meadows Two replaces car parking with two distinct gardens moving the parking to the periphery without loss of spaces. In the centre of each is a grass lawn for community activities with wild meadow planting and shrubs around.

The planting concept works with blocks of plants to generate strong geometries. The strategy is to create two scales of contemplation, from a ground perspective but also from the four towers above.

Private Client, London, UK
Rear Window Extension
house extension, 2006

Rear Window is a collaboration with Anya Gallaccio and Kelly Eginton for the remodeling of a London 1970s house. The project consisted of a large perforation in the rear of the house connecting the garden to the living space. This window was detailed as a frameless opening creating an immediate connection to the garden. The zone between the existing structure and the outdoors was clad with reclaimed roughly planed pine planks with the steel channels within the zone of the wall.

Wood was the key material chosen for this renovation as the project employs seven different types of wood with a wide range of types and finishes (mahogany, birch, oak, maple, cherry, ash and pine). The kitchen cabinet doors were made of the same reclaimed pine wood as the window. The rough plane finish of the reclaimed boards exposes the wear and tear over the years. The living room shelving units were made of birch ply to contrast with the dark reclaimed mahogany flooring. A black board was designed make the kitchen block appear as a piece of furniture sitting on the mahogany floor throughout the entire ground floor kitchen, hall, and living rooms.

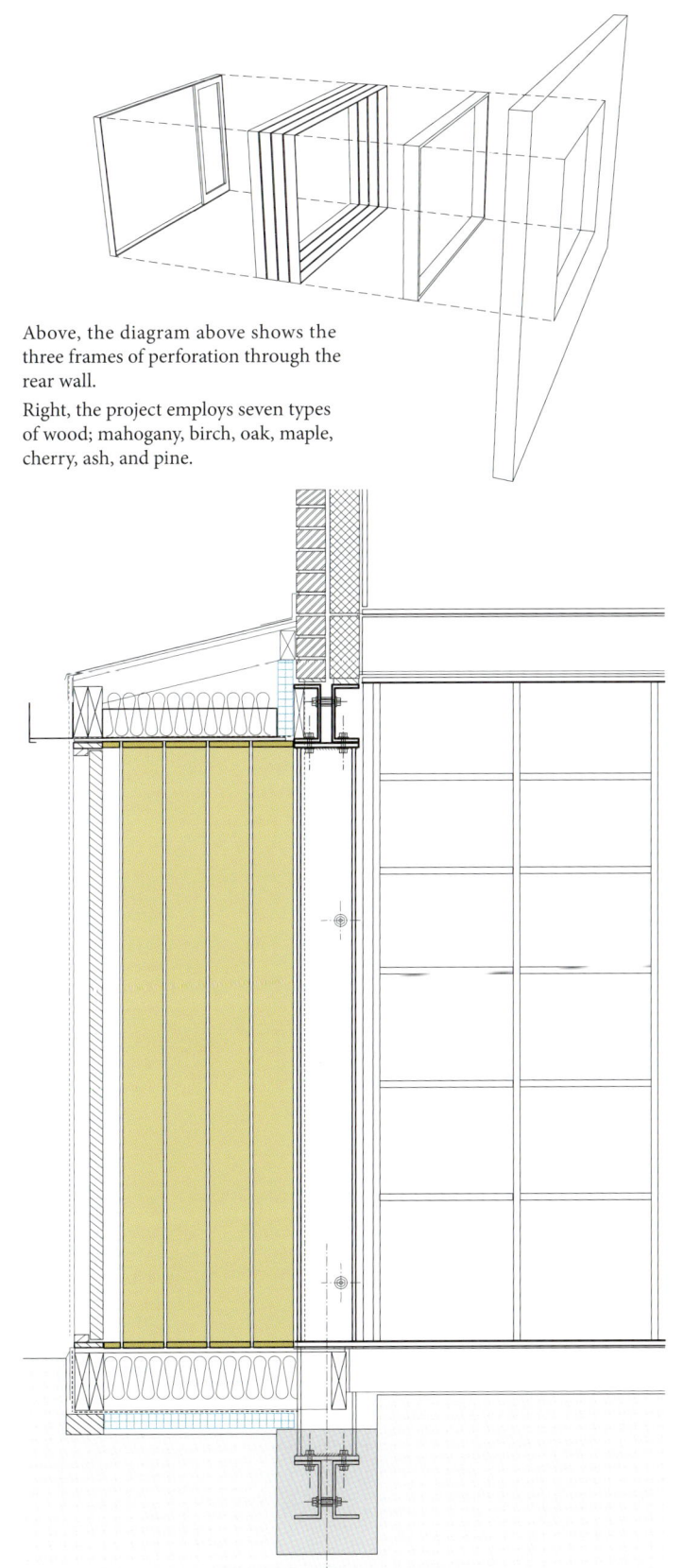

Above, the diagram above shows the three frames of perforation through the rear wall.

Right, the project employs seven types of wood; mahogany, birch, oak, maple, cherry, ash, and pine.

Arch Foundation/ British Land, London, UK
Re-Verse it Plaza
urban plaza, 2007

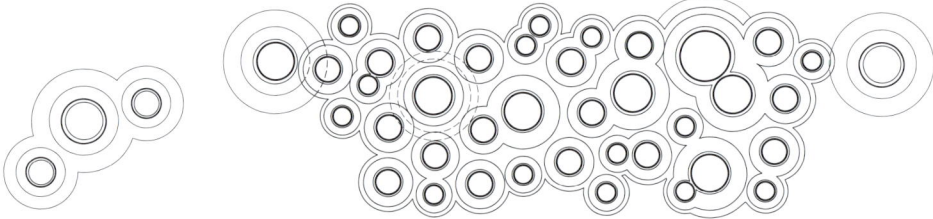

Re-Verse it explores the displacement of domestic objects in an urban context. The upside down flowerpots play with fantasy and imagination making reference to the nearby gardens of Regent's Park. The proposal uses change of scale to create a bold and friendly outdoor environment where these common terracotta flower pots transmute and multiply into seating, tree planters, and a powerful eating canopy for a cafe. This cafe roof was designed to be seen from the offices above creating impact for the workers. As the site had a carpark directly below it, all planting had to contain soil above the pavement in raised beds. We were shortlisted with five other practices to design this new plaza competition at Regent's Place Estate organised by the Architecture Foundation in partnership with British Land. After joint first place and a further submission we were placed second.

The plan (below) shows the the colonisation of the area by differnt pot programmes. Some components radically change the scale and become skylights for a proposed cafe (main picture).

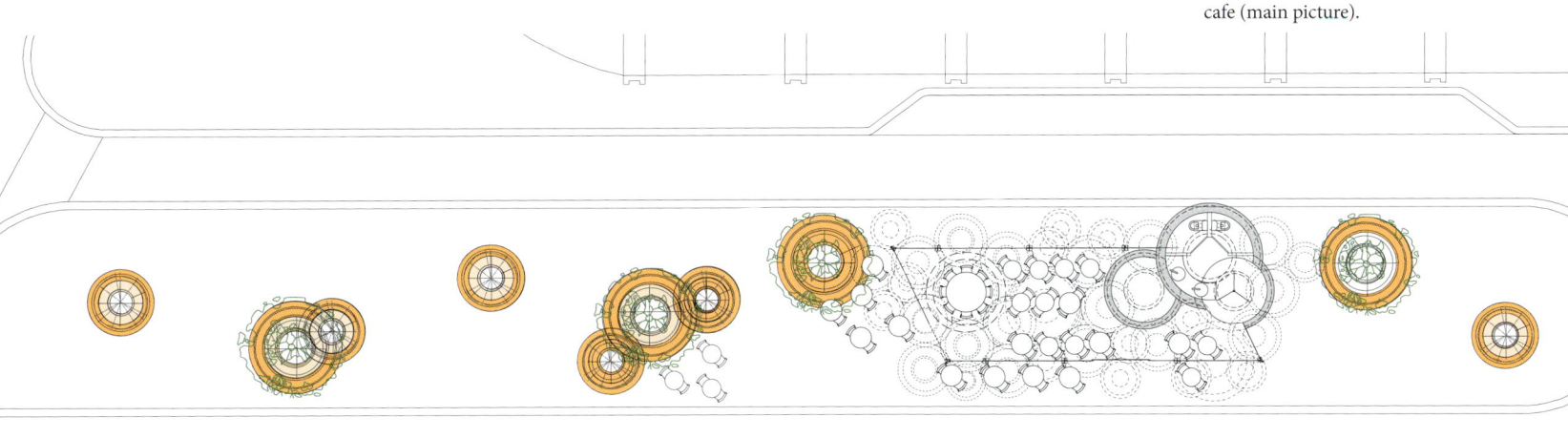

Arch Foundation-Old Street, London, UK
Lunatic Garden

plaza competition, 2004

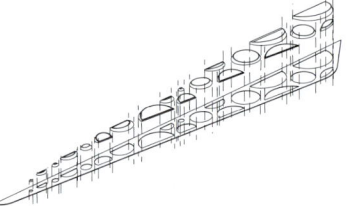

The garden was defined by a series of giant skewed conical planters generating a new topograghy for Old Street.

Lunatic Garden explores extruded perforations of the pavement plane. A landscape of cones are punched up from the ground to become wildflower planters and benches along a busy urban road. It was a competition for the Old Street roundabout, London organised by the Architectural Foundation. The wide pavement allowed for a separation into two zones, a straight route cutting diagonally across the site defined by mapping the direct movement of pedestrians towards the underground entrance, and the garden wedge buffer. The open promenade was designed to allow easy and direct circulation, increase visibility and support to the shops. The garden buffer was designed for social interaction and sitting. Laid out as a more complex pattern of full and part circles, they define a network of curvilinear, meandering paths. These massive concrete cones are tilted at different angles creating seating areas at lower points. The curvilinear walls play with privacy and discovery on the pathways. The plaza was also designed to be seen from the many taller buildings above creating a strong urban impact in the neighbourhood. The old St Luke's Lunatic Hospital previously on the site was a strong reference for the project as lunacy has been associated with the moon. These full and phased moons are, thus appropriate for this site. The scheme proposed to further extend across to the other side and do away with the traffic roundabout.

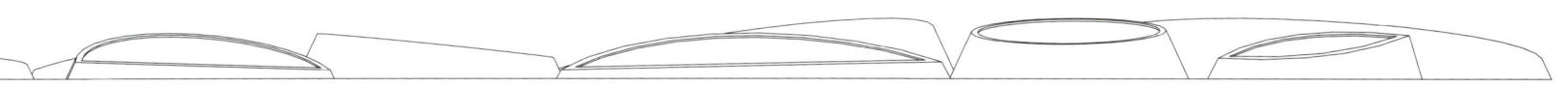

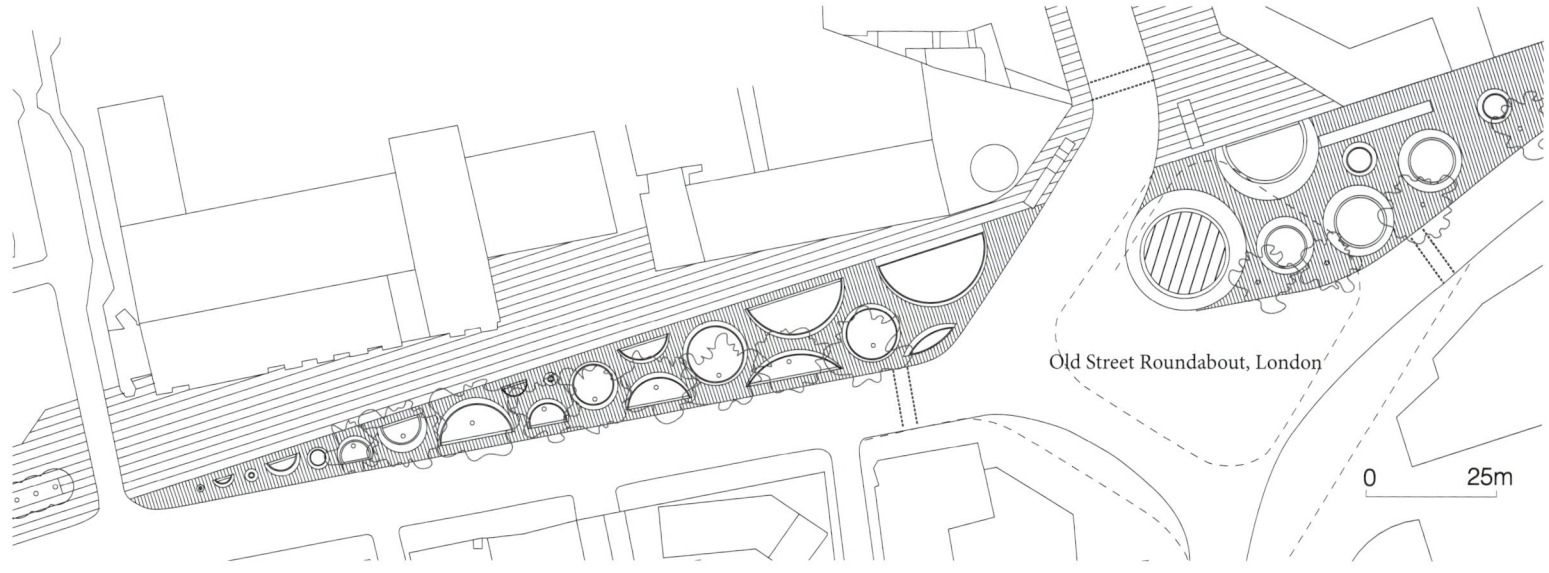

Old Street Roundabout, London

0   25m

Float

Exploring a Sense of Weightlessness

Float interests us as it is an action that will inevitably suggest weightlessness and ephemerality, qualities we regularly pursue in our work. Float is the most ethereal spatial verb in this book as it is intrisically related to experience and phenomenology. It explores our ability to read spatial information through our senses. The vestibular and proprioceptive senses really interest us, senses that are related to movement, speed, balance, and gravity. It is a question of exploring space looking at the body in motion in relation to orientation, time, and speed.

Float is about the vertical dimension, the emphasis on the exploration of the Z axis. It immediately relates to the experience of lightness and loss of gravity and it is the action that is most likely to reconcile the virtual and the real world. The illusion of weightlessness is usually achieved by the exploration of structural delicacy or structural instability, materiality, and the depiction of movement. Structural delicacy is a question of economy and efficiency looking at the minimum effort required. It pushs the limits of a structure to its maximum potential. Structural instability brings time into the equation as it gives the sensation of structural unpredictability suggesting a sense of flux and ephemerality. Objects and buildings can be dematerialsed by the use of transparent, translucent and see-through materials. This chapter shows a series of projects that pursue lightness and depict weightlessness. Float is usually explored in our work with complementary actions such as layering or stacking.

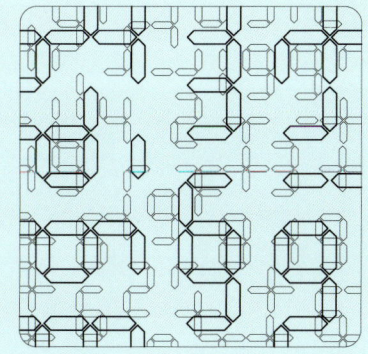

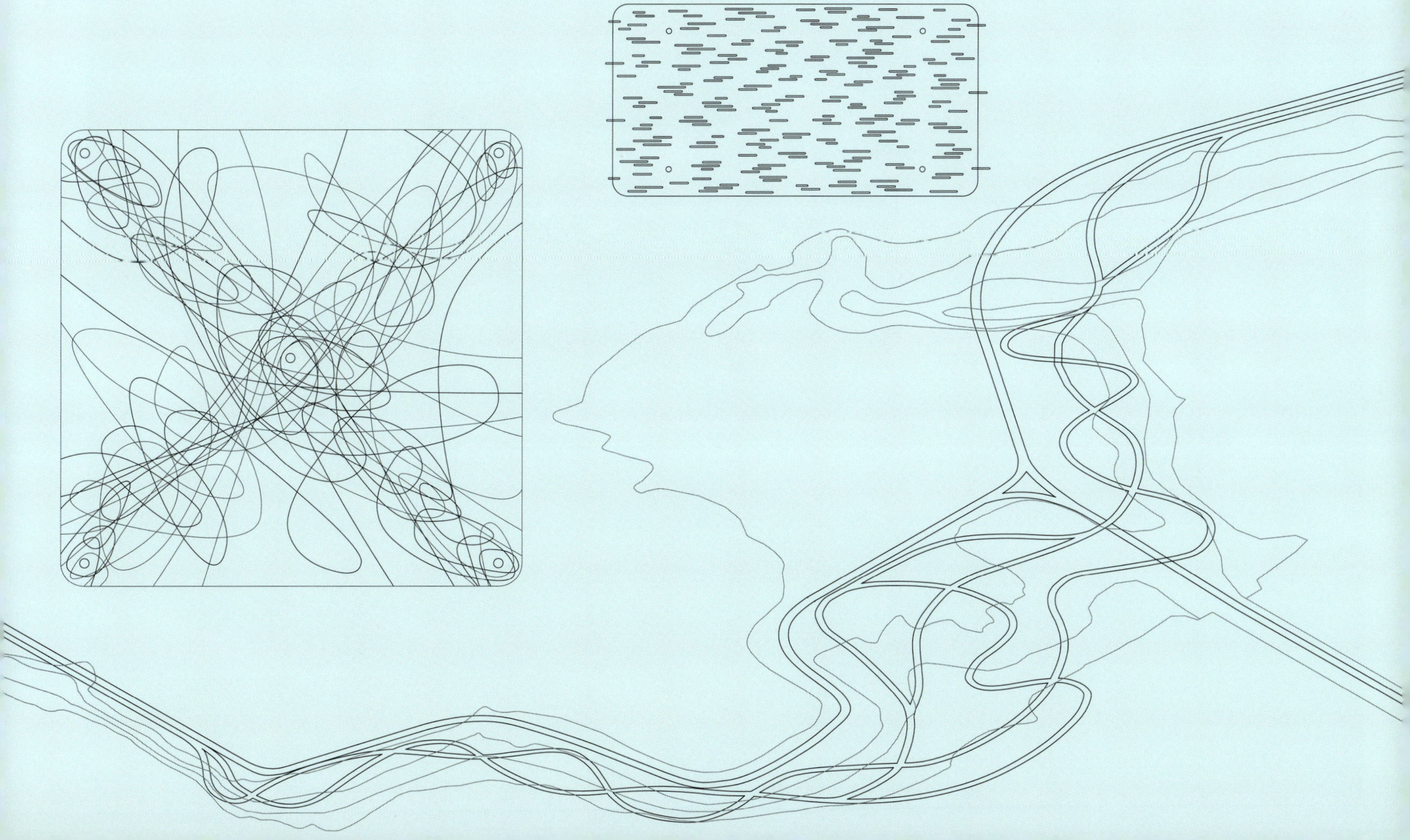

RHS Chelsea Flower Show, London, UK

Tableau Garden

RHS GOLD Medal, large show garden, 2000

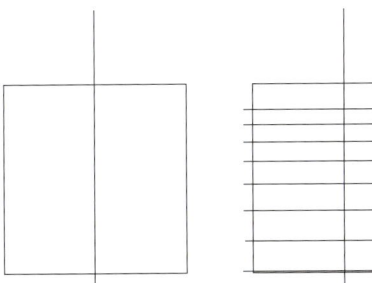 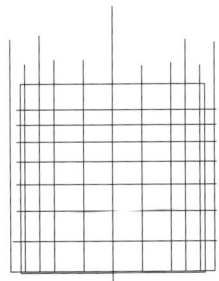 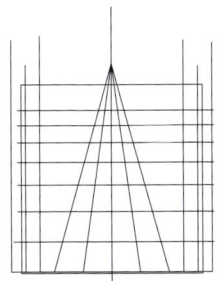 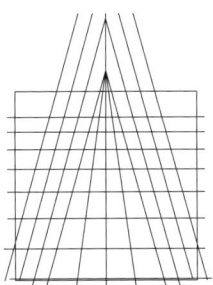 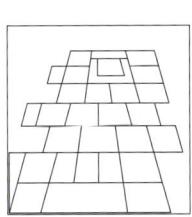

Tableau "Jardin sans Frontières" at the Royal Horticulture Show, Chelsea, 2000, explores forced perspective and spatial illusions. The concept was based on a Renaissance theatre design where the tableau is a distorted grid built with one viewing point to create an illusion of space through forced perspective. This approach suits Chelsea as show gardens can only be viewed from the public path. The forced pespective is accentuaded by escalating the plateaus in height towards the back. The grid, with its regular modules, allowed the grouping of different specimens of ornamental cabbages, herbs, and flowers by theme or colour. Varieties of vegetable plants were mixed with flowers suggesting a new type of garden where contemplation meets consumption. Two glass kiosks and a glass bridge float above the planting and watercourse. We collaborated with Rhyl Knowles commissioned by two English and French gardens sponsored by the European Union for Chelsea Flower Show. Winner of a RHS Gold medal in 2000.

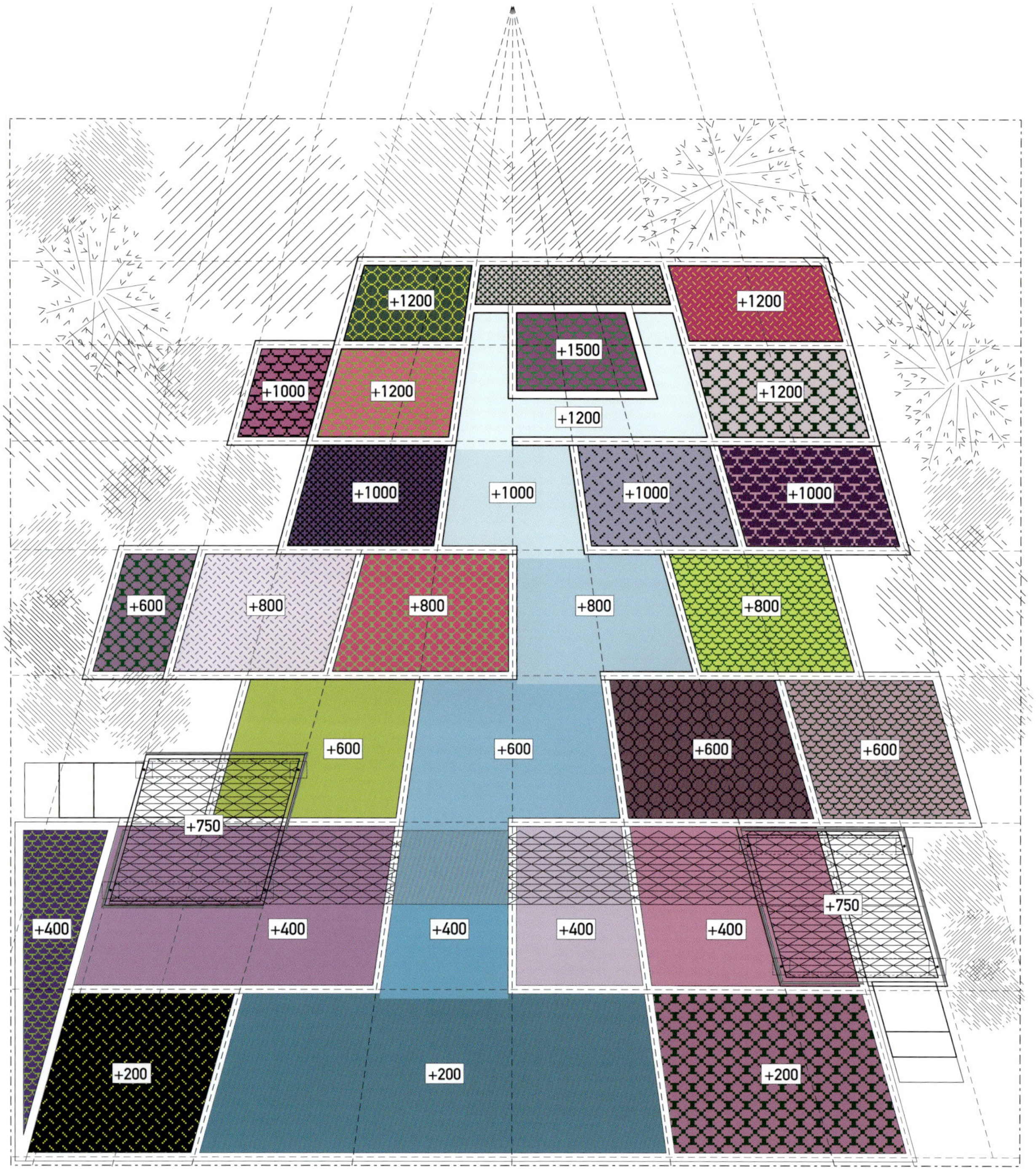

+1200
+1200
+1000
+1200
+1500
+1200
+1200
+1000
+1000
+1000
+1000
+1000
+600
+800
+800
+800
+800
+600
+600
+600
+600
+750
+400
+400
+400
+400
+400
+750
+200
+200
+200

A water feature meanders down a strip of central blocks with water falling at each level change. A glass bridge connects across the galvanised metal walkway grill which floats above the planting. The forced perspective design created diamond shaped terraces and kiosks with an illusion of space in the small garden.

Scribble / Splash / Web Tables

limited edition, 1998–2002

Scribble explores customised engraving processes allowing a variety of designs in limited production runs. The technique interests us as it defines an object by its boundary and not by its mass. Depth and tri-dimensionality are achieved on 2-D surfaces.

Different engraving techniques were tested on 2 mm acrylic slabs creating contrasting visual effects and illusions through multiple reflections. The use of a V groove floating router creates a gradual difference in the thickness of the line produced as the acrylic varies in thickness as a cast object. Laser cutting produces precise etched lines and cut through voids.

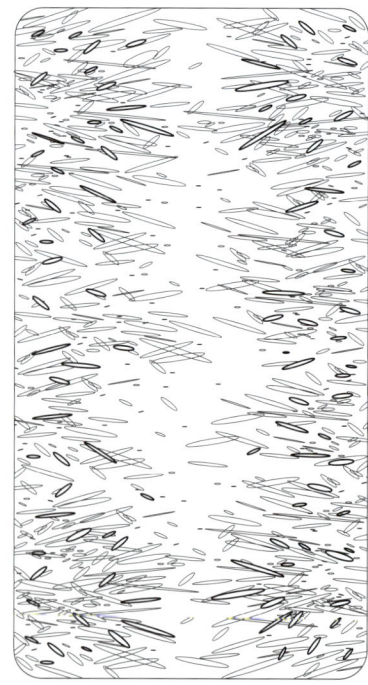

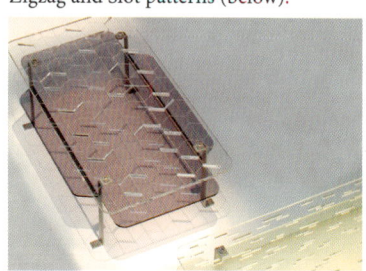

One-offs in 2000 with Splash (right), Zigzag and Slot patterns (below).

A limited production of six tables were produced of four Web (left), one Scribble (middle) and for Colette, Paris one 1999 pattern (right). Patterns were computer numeric control routed V grooves on top and bottom surfaces creating reflections. Web in bottom photo.

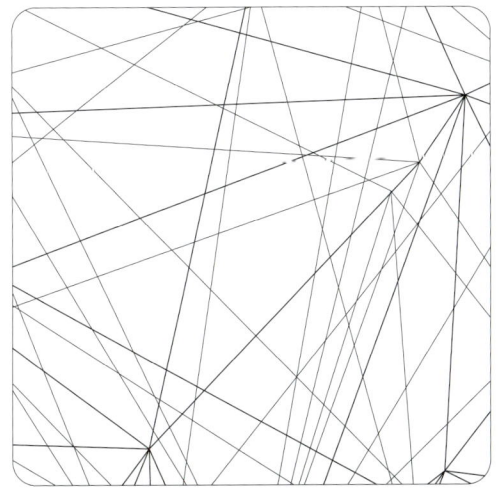 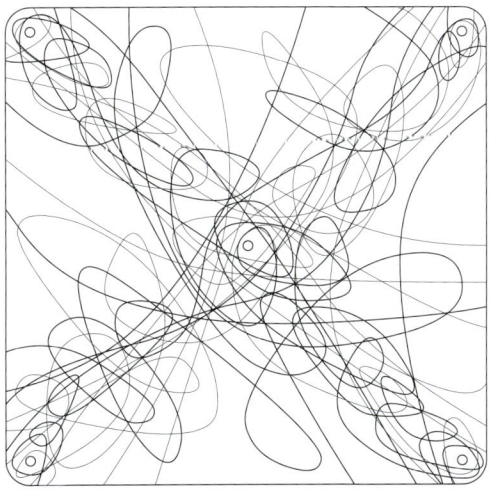 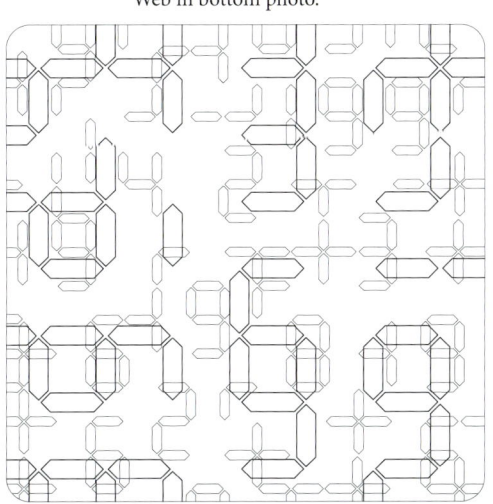

Colette, Paris, France
Pixel Counter
one-off nailbar, 1997

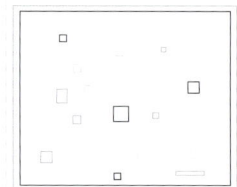 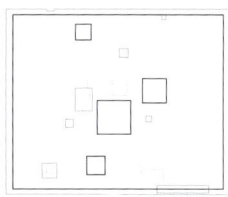 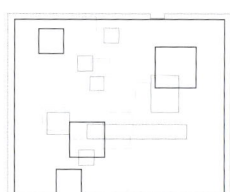 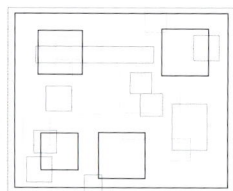 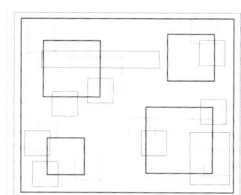

Comme des Garçons shop blue partitions in Joyce Department Store, Hong Kong.

Pixel explores visual depth and tri-dimensional effects on 2-D planes. A series of squares were cut in 3 mm acrylic layers and sandwiched together with 1 mm toughened glass top and bottom. The overlay of three satin finish layers created a shimmering floating effect to the pattern emphasising depth. The satin finish blurs the deepest layers creating ghosting and reflections. The project was a special commission nail bar counter for the Colette shop in Paris in 1997.

Joyce Panels, a simlar commission in 1998 of large three metre long panels for Comme des Garçons in the Joyce Department Store, Hong Kong. Four large blue panels were hung as partitions to create identity to the brand in the larger department store. A translucent dark blue tint was chosen mixed with white satin frost layers. The ghosting effects were more pronounced with the blue.

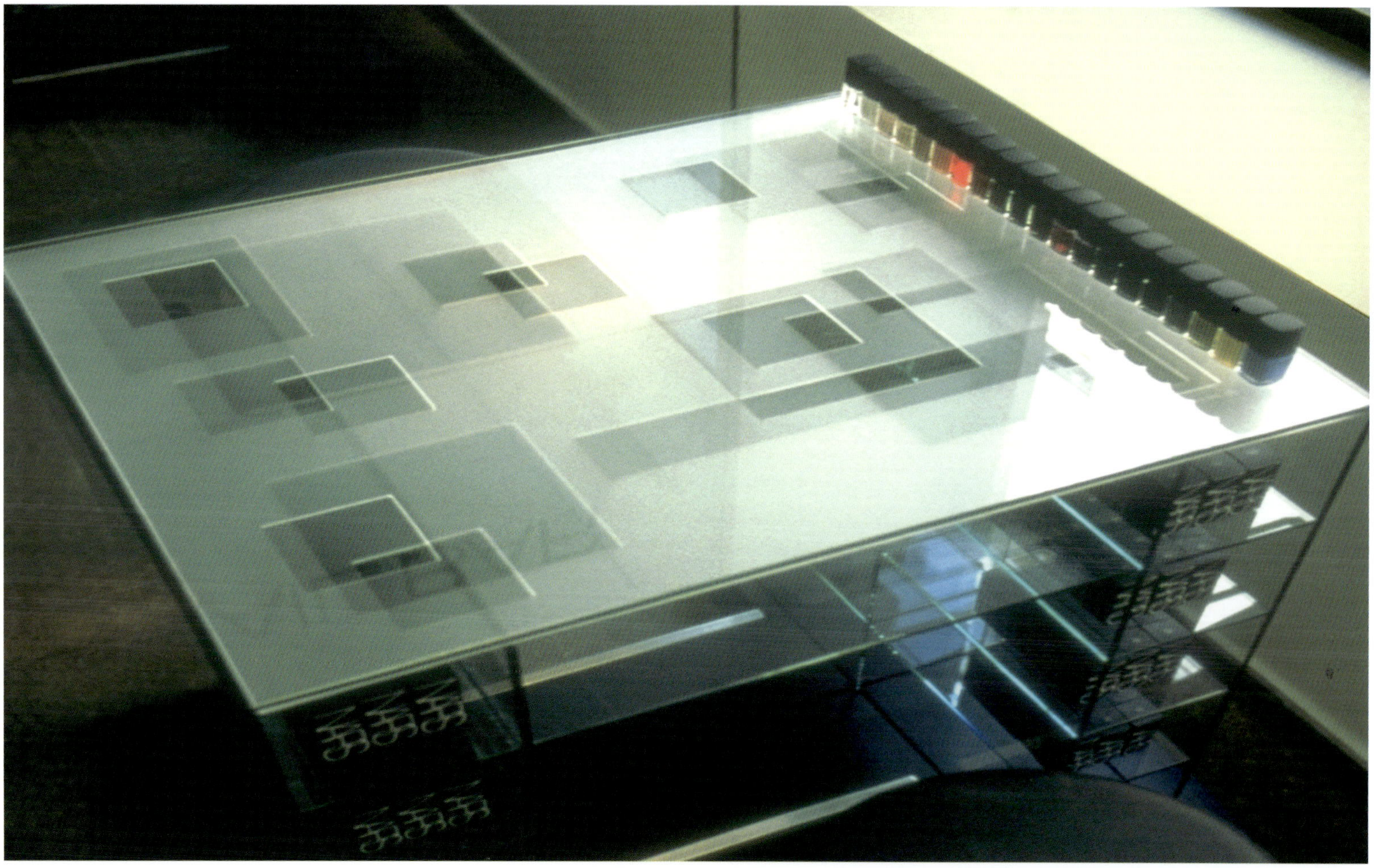

Domino Storage

prototype storage system units, 2006

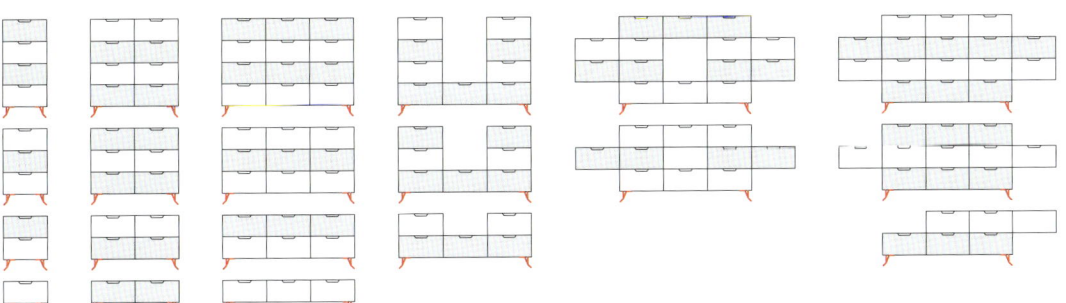

Domino explores multiple layout configurations of a stackable storage system. The design allows different arrangements and configurations of one, two, or three drawer units assembled in different ways by the user.

The design embraces the edge of the material exposed as an expression of the cutting process of the CNC technology. Originally seen as a "mistake" by the manufacturer, the material property of melamine laminated MDF sheets was used as an opportunity within the manufacturing process. Rounded edges expose the inner MDF at corners which break each drawer as a distinct block. The three unit pieces are made to be cantilevered on top and across other pieces. Unlike most storage pieces, the Domino has four finished sides so it can be displayed as a central element in the room.

Two three units with cantilevered top.

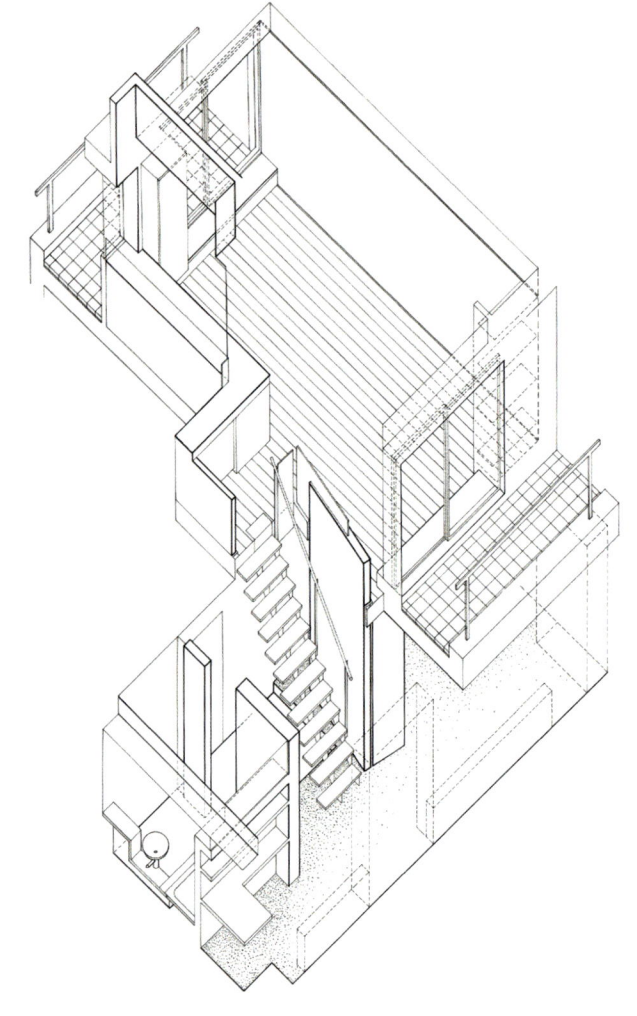

Private Client, Soho, London UK
Bento Box Apartment
penthouse,1995

Bento Box explores flexibility of a small residential space in central London to create a sense of openness and fluidity. Hidden doors, when closed against cupboards, allow the entry hall to flow into the bedroom. Flush windows, without returns, extend perceived wall lengths such as at the kitchen window and skylight. A bathroom internal frosted glass door and corner slot allow the hall and bathroom to blend. This is further emphasised by the eight large bathroom marble floor slabs which extend out into the hall. Above the shower, a slot window, flush to the ceiling borrows light from the study beyond. The stairway opens vertically and diagonally leading one up into the living space. This 5th and 6th floor penthouse is taller than other Soho buildings allowing for views above London from both east and west terraces. The renovation flipped the spaces and colonised part of the large east roof terrace to increase the living room space. As one walks up the stairs, the kitchen slot window frames St Giles Church. The marble slab fridge block floats above the cherry floor and makes conversation with Centre Point in the background. Bento Box was the first Procter-Rihl commission.

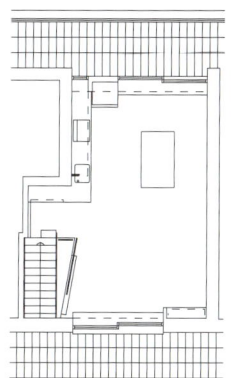

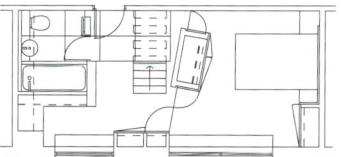

A tilted central storage block sits in the midddle of the entry floor. Side panels fold out as doors to close the bedroom.

Private Client, London, UK
Shift Housing
urban infill four residential units, 2003

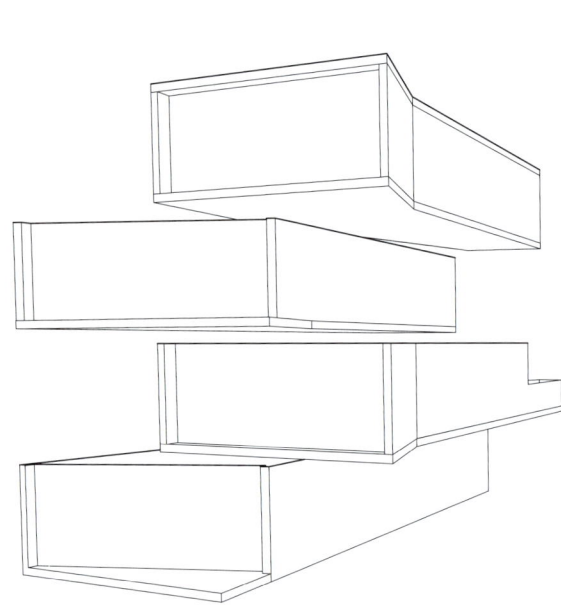

Shift explores a sense of movement and speed in a residential building. The triangular site abuts car parking to north and east with the street to the west and rail tracks running on the south perimeter. It is a freestanding building that was formly a Victorian warehouse. Only the base storey currently exists of the former brick three-storey structure. As the clients overlook the site, they purchased it as they wanted to control their view and screen the trains. Each of the three flats and the ground floor office are stacked above each other and designed as independent vessels composed of contrasting materials (wood, stone, brick and metal cladding). The floors are shifted and appear as independent linear strips reflecting the movement of the trains. Privacy and overshadowing of neighbouring sites were also key design language generators. Boundary wall windows were placed within triangular cuts into the facade with the window facing away from the neighbouring housing. The shifted blocks created deep overhangs, used as sun control balconies, or occasionally on the north, as skylights.

The project also responds to the issue of sound from the trains to one side. This facade has no windows and is shielded by a four-storey external stair structure. The stairwall is clad with perforated metal producing dappled daylight and the diffusion of sound.

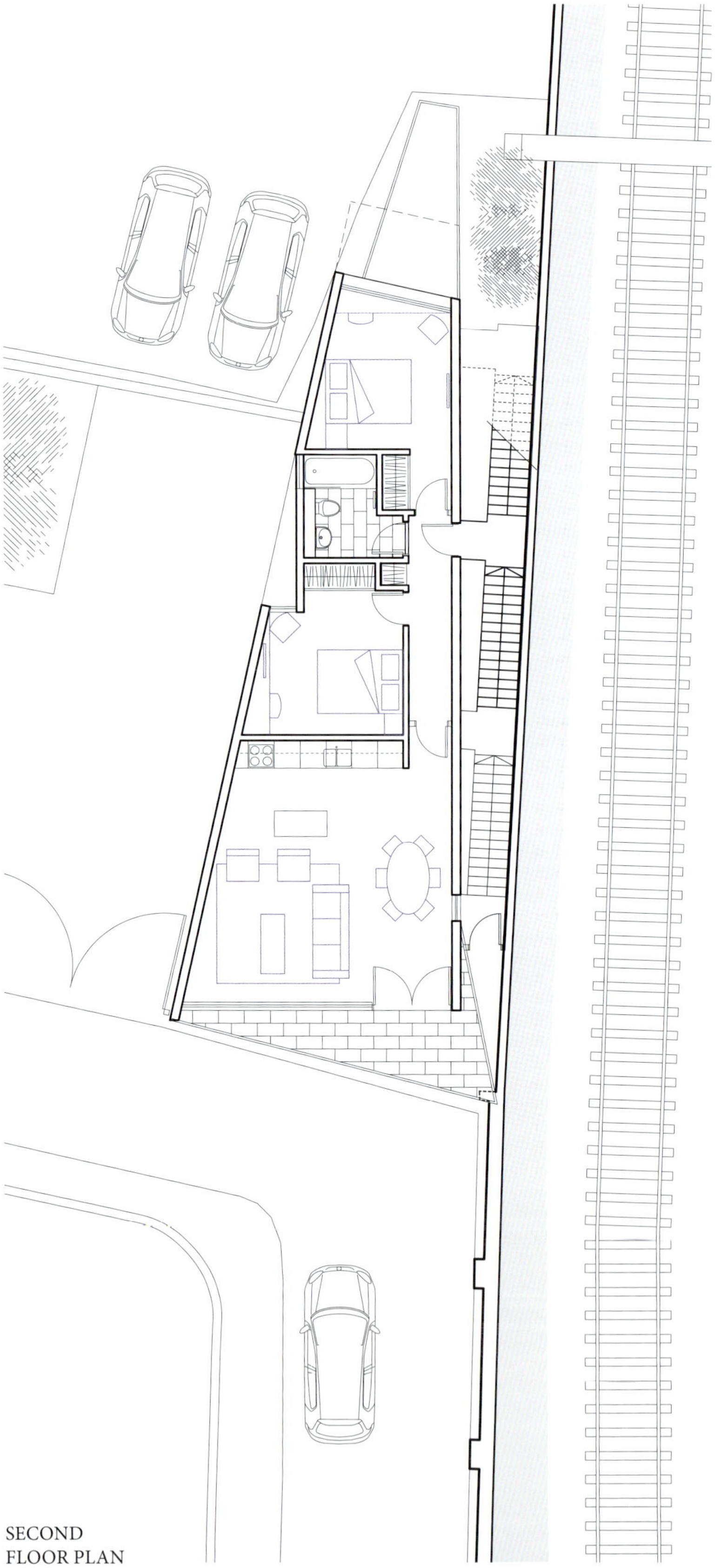

SECOND
FLOOR PLAN

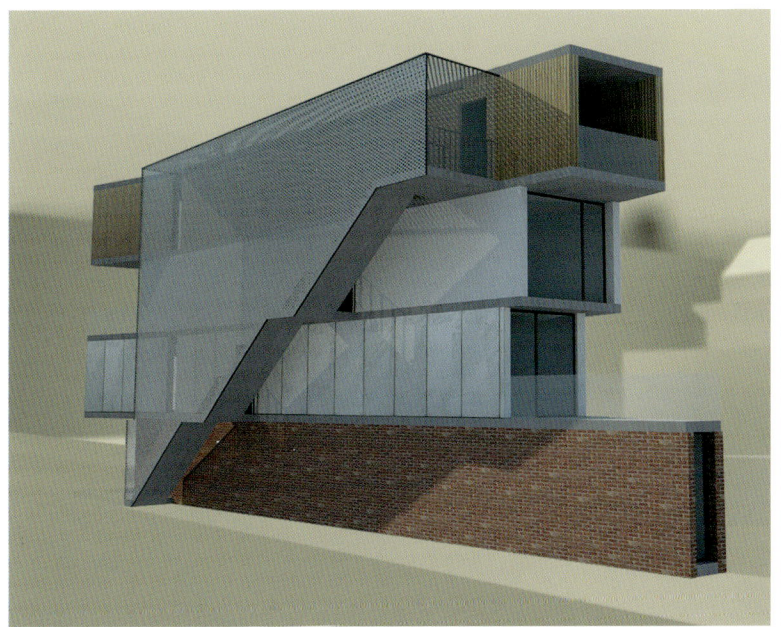

The stairwell is an independent object attached to the main building clad with perforated mesh to allow a soft filtered light into the space.

Private Client, Porto Alegre, Brazil
Nonoai House
new residence, 2016

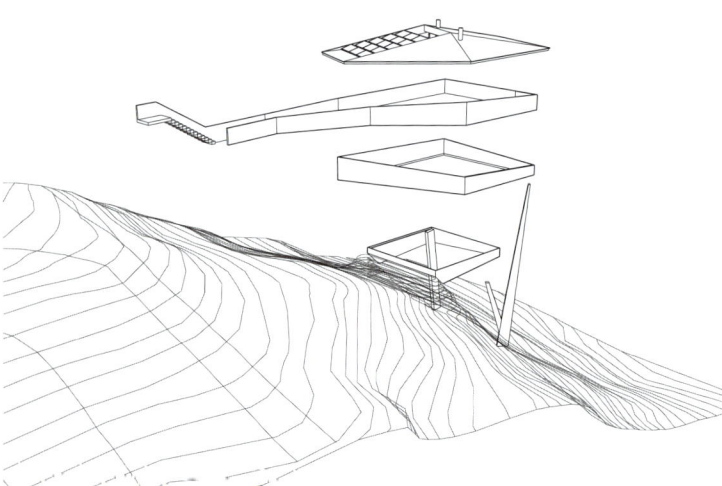

Nonoai explores a sense of weightlessness and ephemerality. The site is located at the top of Nonoai mount which overlooks the city and nearby river. It shares its site boundaries with a forested nature reserve. The studio decided not to intervene in the site topography, raising the house on concrete legs to take advantage of the views. The house sits on the edge of the site propped up by two tilted concrete columns which pierce through internal spaces. The social area is at the highest level accessible from a floating bridge that connects the garage at the top of the site to the main structure. The private areas were placed in the two lower levels.

The project employs many environment strategies such as large overhanging roof shading, outdoor deck, adjustable exterior louvres and few windows on the sunny north facade, insulated structure, rain water cisterns and solar electric roof panels. The building has been oriented directly north to maximise daylighting and solar collection.

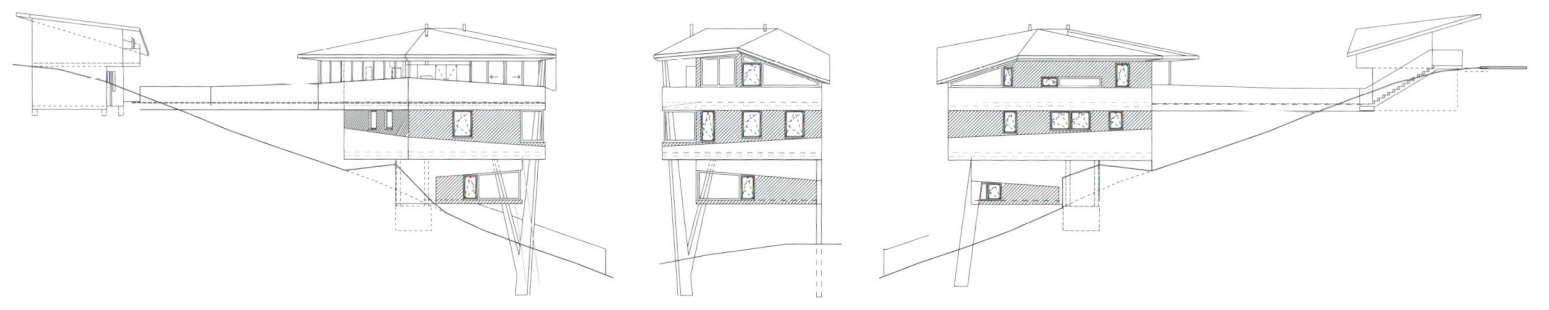

A series of skewed concrete bands wrap around the building creating an illusion of continous loops in the space and emphasising horizontal planes. Infill areas are clad with handmade glass mosaics in strong colours breaking the volume as horizontal bands. The upper level living room is shaped by a folded roof creating interesting internal geometries. The house has extended eaves and louvres towards the west to protect from solar radiation. The structure is pierced by tilted columns creating a dialogue between inside and outside.

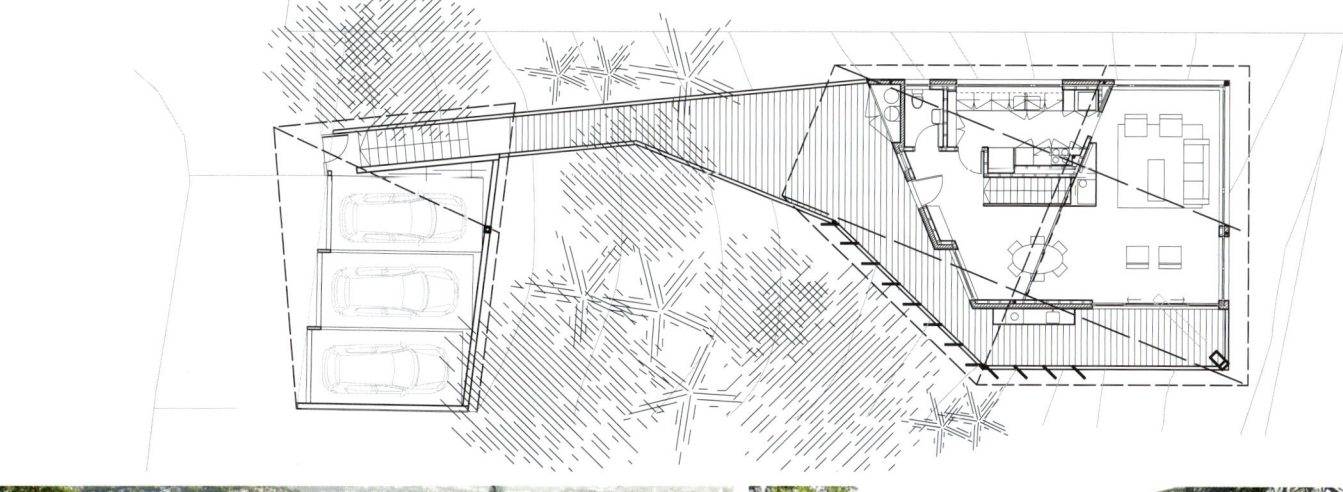

Leisure Programmes
A - Pedestrian Promenade / Floating Platforms
B - Cycle lanes / Floating platforms
C - Pop-up Events

Production Programmes
D - Tree Nursery
E - Water Filtering Ponds
F - Fish Hatchery

Palafita Park

new sustainable urban park, 2013

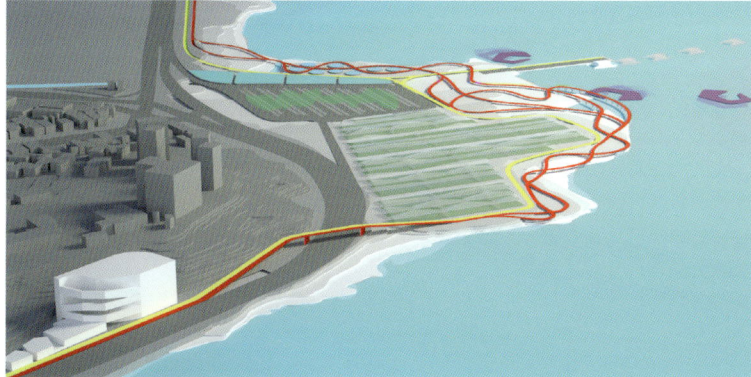

Aerial view of Palafita Park with Siza designed art museum.

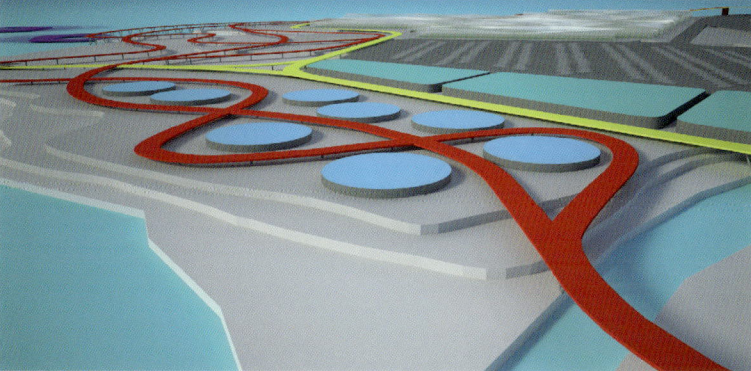

Water filtering ponds and fish hatchery.

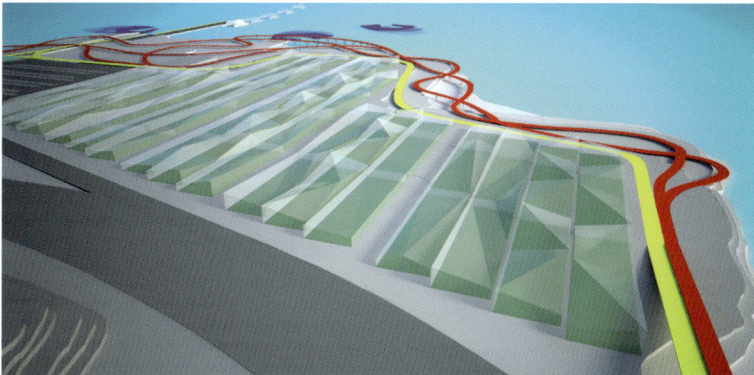

Tree nurseries, pedestrian and cycle lanes.

Floating programmes and pop-up events.

Palafita is a research project questioning the privatisation of the public spaces in Brazilian cities. The project is a reflection of a one week workshop in collaboration with PROPAR/ UFRGS (Programa de Pós Graduação em Arquitetura UFRGS-Universidade Federal do Rio Grande do Sul, Brazil). The workshop functioned as an arena for discussions to enable Procter-Rihl to develop a design proposal for the site.

The 53,000 m² area reflects a typical city strategy of continual landfill extension into the river bed. The area was originally riverbed until 1949 when the "Shipyard So" transferred to this peninsula after the massive flood of that year which raised water levels above 4.5 metres in Porto Alegre. In 1974, the production reached 170 boats with 1,500 employees. In 1995, the shipyard went into bankruptcy due to the lack of fiscal incentives and low market demand. There are remains of the shipyard on site with the old pier. Today, the site has a prominent position as it sits between the longest park in the city and a new urban development area with shopping malls, large residential blocks, a race course, sailing clubs, and a new super sewage station.

The design tackles future environmental concerns, such as the rise of water levels in our rivers through architectural expression. The park accepts and embraces future river level rises by proposing light weight mobile, pre-fab constructions or by raising certain programmes above river levels. The ground is left native and untouched. The proposal suggests a new park typology where production and leisure are woven together, environmental factory meeting leisure programmes. Three key "production" programmes (tree nursery, fish hatcheries, water treatment ponds) becomes accessible to the city woven with leisure programmes (floating promenade and floating pods for pop-up events and non pre-determined activities.

Production Programmmes

- Tree Nursery – to supply the city with native species and distribute them to the general public to promote the importance of diversity of local species.
- Fish Hatchery – to produce native species and feed them back into the river.
- Water Filtering Ponds - a proposal of a series of filtering ponds with reeds to absorb pollution filtering the water in a passive manner. The ponds sit at different heights to encourage oxygenation of the water from the river above. The ponds aim to treat the water effluents with a series of filtering pools and "Aguapes" plants. "Aguapes" are plants originally from the Amazon that are able to filter water. They absorb and accumulate pollution filtering the water in a passive manner.

Leisure Programmes

- Pedestrian Promenade /Floating Platforms - The pedestrian route starts from the white concrete Ibere Camargo Museum (Alvaro Siza architect) as an intertwined double route. When it reaches its central area it starts to generate a concentric journey suggesting a wander around a "virtual square". The pedestrian routes float around 2 m to 3 m above the ground in the flood zone.
- Floating Programmes / pop-up events / non pre-determined activities - The floating platforms can anchor to specific areas in the site. They have the dual function of a floating hatchery for distribution of new stocks in the river Guaiba but also can host pop-up events and other leisure activities during the year.
- Cycle lanes - An extension of the park cycle lanes to connect with the new development on the south of the park. The cycle lanes have an independent route but occasionally meet the pedestrian walkways.

The project is a homage to Jose Lutzemberger, the first internationally known Brazilian environmentalist. Sustainable programmes are made visible to the general public and woven together with leisure to become a strong symbol for the city.

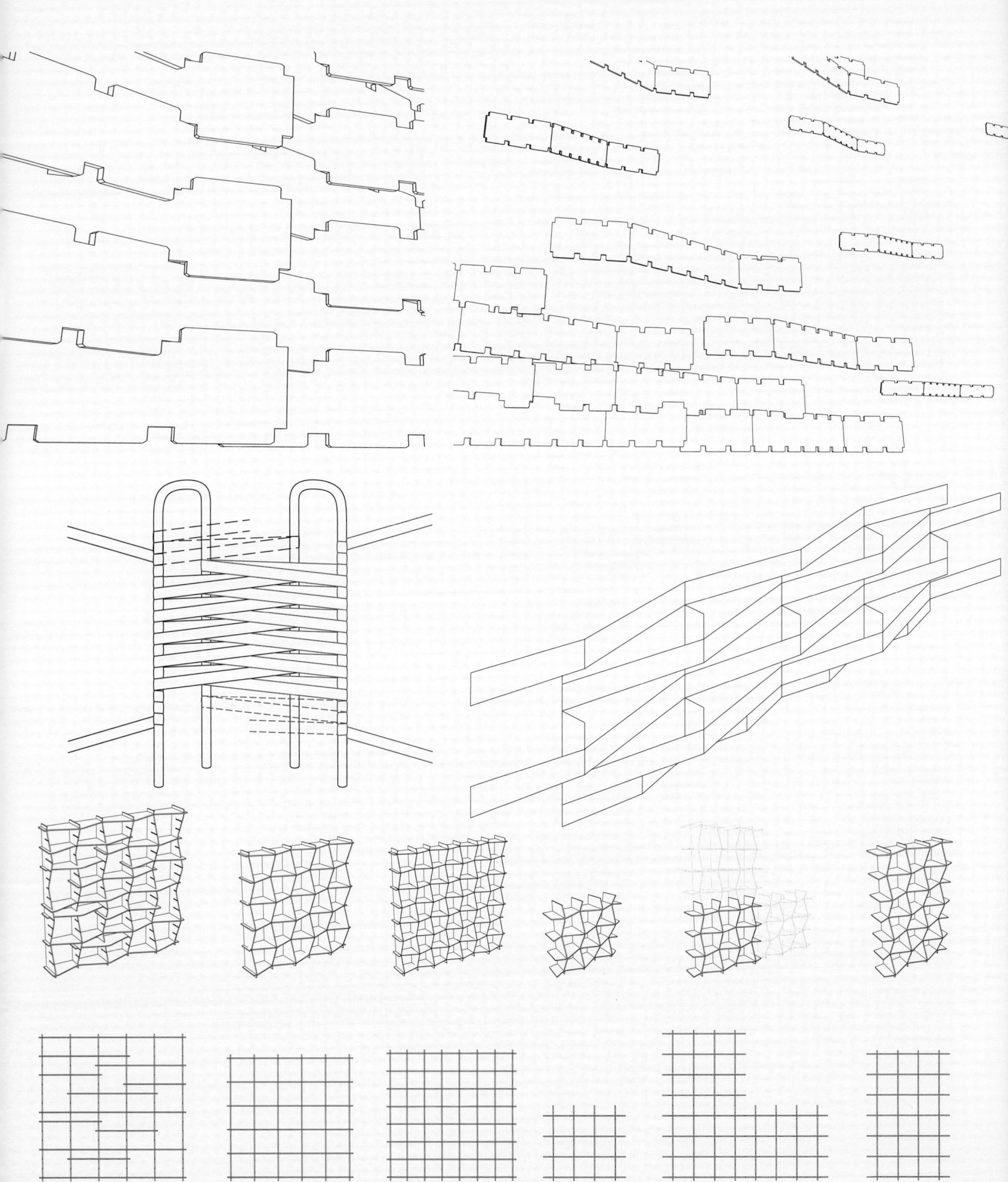

Weave

Exploring a Sense of Continuity

Weave interests us as an action as it evokes a sense of continuity where space becomes boundaryless. Some projects employ this action in a literal manner, others are developed by looking at its variants, also defined as interlacing, knitting, braiding, plaiting intertwining or zig-zagging. Some projects work on a principle of suggestion by depicting a woven structure such as the Topo project, for example on pages 106, 107.

Weave is an action that immediately relates to the field of craft and making. The studio is interested in craft and making as cultural expressions of a place and its relationship to the body, concept, material and production. Craft reveals how a specific culture solves problems in everyday life, engages with materials and expresses aesthetic concerns. In most cultures, making is related to survival where innovation happens due to necessity. Solutions are evolutionary and transformational edited by trial and error, only becoming an established practice through time.

We are interested in exploring craft and making through possibilites and limitations of the craft processes. These opportunities include analysis of errors and mistakes in the production process. The studio is interested in fusing innovation to an established craft process. Innovation would inevitably happen through investigations, analysis and exploratory tests of the processes in question. Innovation will occur by an alternative way of working, radical change of scale, material or tools. Sometimes, it is about mixing unusual materials not usually associated together or by using an unexpected material in a traditional process. Weave is usually explored in our work with complementary actions such as Twist, Bend and Stitch.

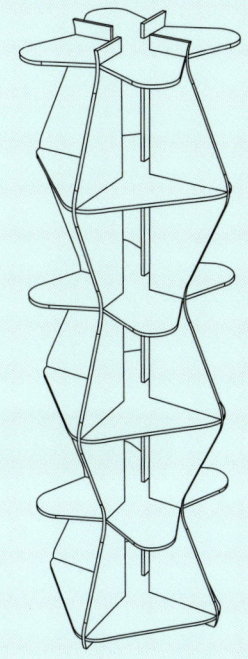

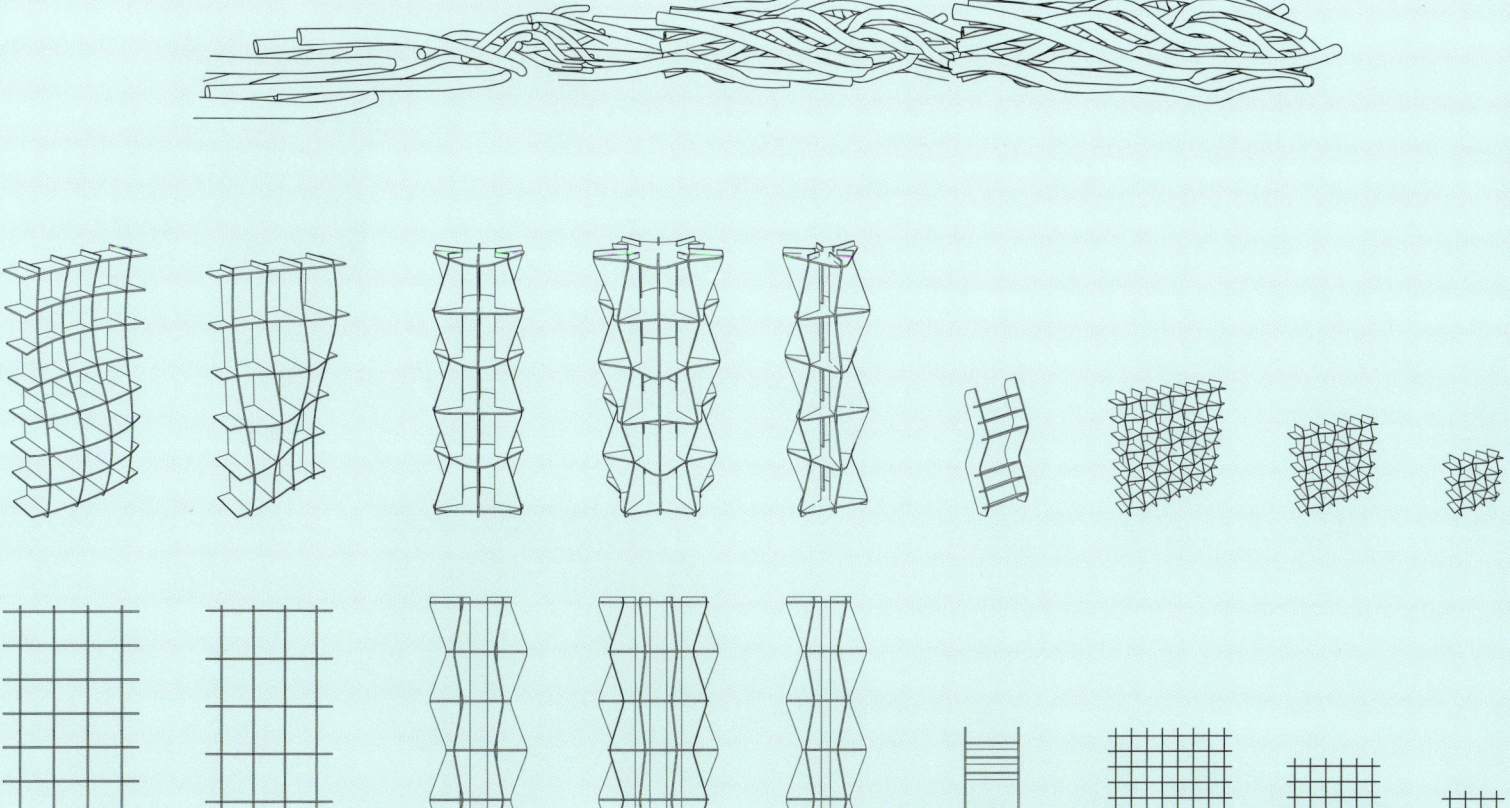

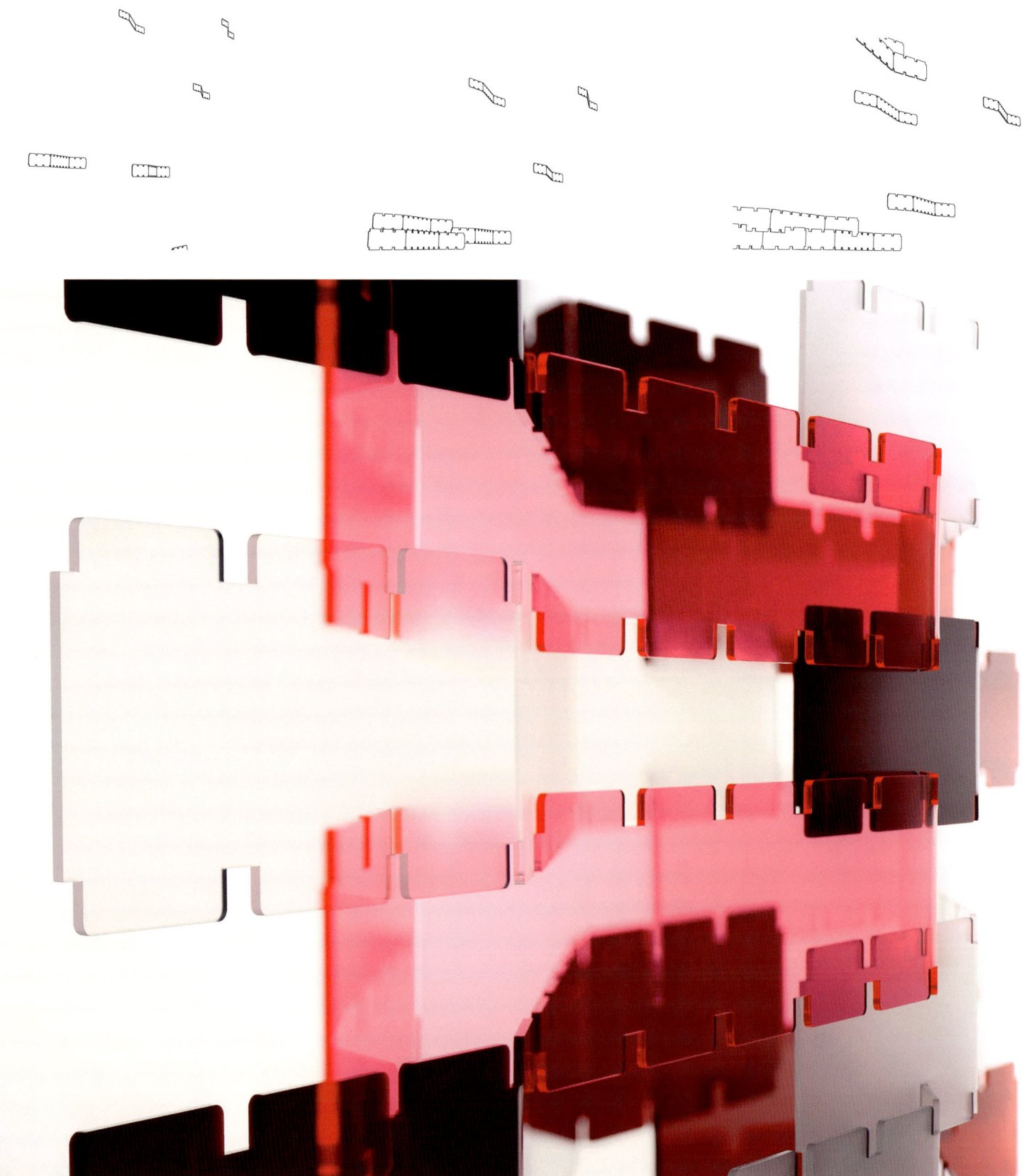

Super8 and Kaleidoscope Screens

limited edition screens, 2002, 1999

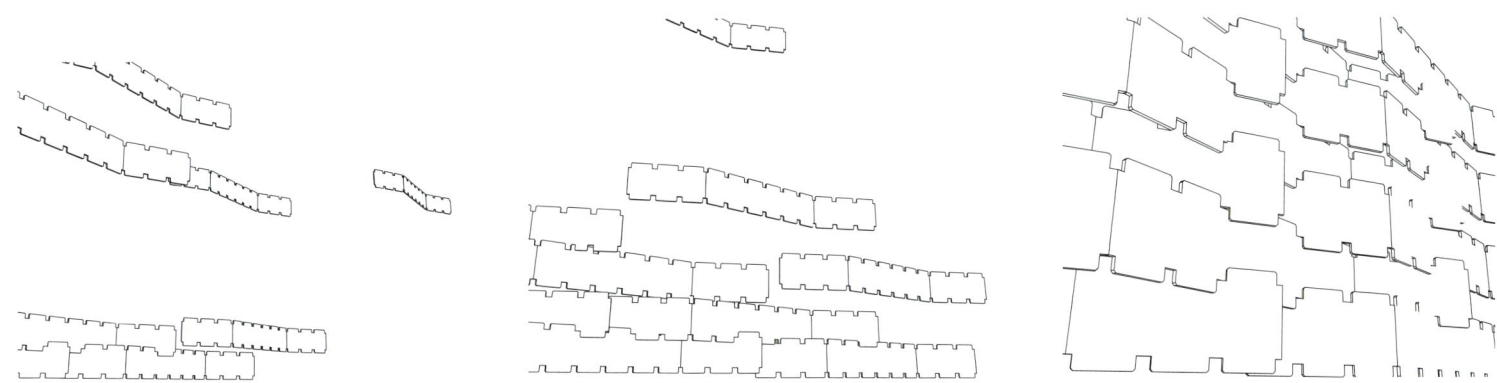

Super8 explores the concept of flexibility through the development of a folded stackable component. Different colour acrylic bands slot together to create a vertical partition. The user is invited to create different formations by assemblying the components in different configurations. The pieces were made in three different finishes: frost, translucent and live edge. All pieces were lasercut and hand folded. The Z singular component allows different stretched or wide woven configurations. The piece has no fixings, just a series of regular nibs that interlock together and resemble old film strips. Super8 is a development of a previous design, the **Kaleidoscope** screen which was made as a limited edition of five screens in 1999. These are rectangular folded acrylic pieces riveted together into S-shaped curves fixed as two panels between metal uprights hinged in the middle.

Cocada Preta, Brazil
Strap Chair
limited edition chairs, 2005–2014

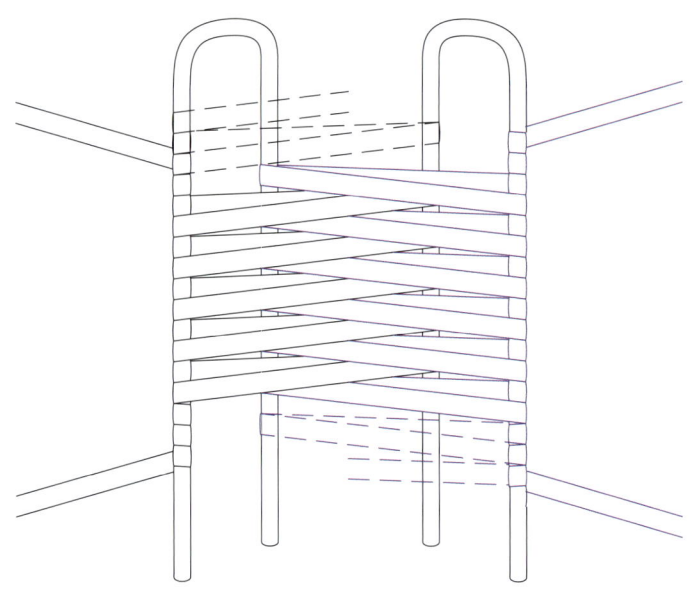

Strap is a lightweight chair with nylon straps weaving diagonally through a double-looped frame. The chair is stripped to the minimum amount of components of only structure and woven straps. The double skeleton made of hollow brushed stainless steel tubes allows the weave to become a three-dimensional X-shape responding to an ergonomicaly shaped seat and back. A series of prototypes were made exploring high-back wing chairs (page 16), lounge, cafe chairs, and high stools.

Cobogó Housing

Habitacao Para Todos, social housing competition, 2010

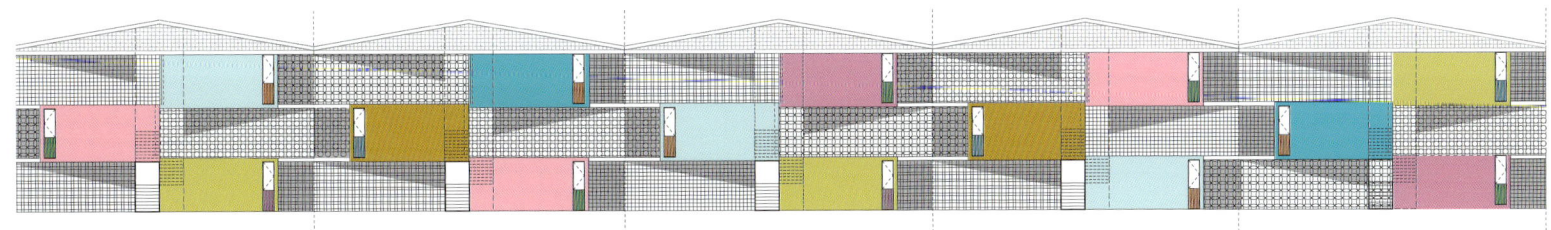

Around a garden square (above) and on a sloped site (below).

Cobogó explores an undulating zigzag facade of alternating solid coloured panels with permeable cobogó cast louvre panels for a Brazilian low income housing competition. Environmental strategies drove this project, with a layout to encourage cross-ventilation through the facades to courtyards, the open entry stairs, and the vented rooves. It employs a traditional Brazilian louvre system in different scales and geometries. The component name, cobogó comes from the initials of three Brazilian engineers who developed the concept of a louvre block to balance internal daylight levels and encourage ventilation at the beginning of the twentieth century. It was originally available in terracota but made widely available in cast concrete. The perforated surfaces on the balconies shade the walls reducing overheating and glare. This continuous street facade typology adapts to different sites and avoids the fragmentation of the urban block, a typical problem of modernist Brazilian urban planning. The proposal is at low human scale for a large housing scheme with shared entries for only six apartments with street parking, garden squares and extensive planting.

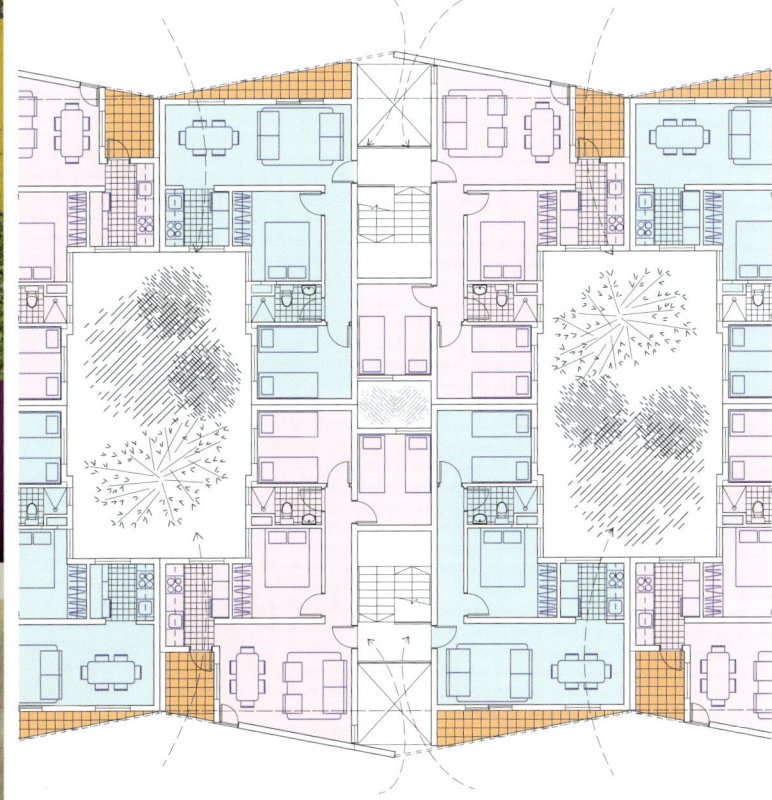

2nd floor three-bedroom apartment   2nd floor two-bedroom apartment

A101 Block City Competition, Moscow, Russia
Urban Weave

urban housing block, 2010

Urban Weave explores an undulating facade animated by shadows produced by the regular weaving of recessed balconies and coloured strips. This three-dimensional facade presents different views depending on your viewing angle of the facade.

The Russian competition brief was based on the principle that the urban grid based city block can be developed with standard units that can be repeated and able to fit any site or orientation. It challenged us to think about adapting a "one size fits all" criteria, contradictory to our beliefs in the development of architecture, to allow the possibility of contextual variety. Our scheme proposal is based on a 25 m square module (see diagram to the right) which allows for flexible block sizes. Each module has a separate entry for only six apartments which creates a sense of security and sub-community within a much larger block structure. All apartments also have three exterior orientations through the use of an inner courtyard allowing daylight and cross-ventilation for any possible block orientation (diagram above).

The design optimises daylight and ventilation. The block would be most effective at 45 degrees north so it neutralises the worst case scenario (north orientation / north hemisphere). Courtyards were designed on equal height to width ratio so even flats on the lower ground level would not be affected by loss of daylight.

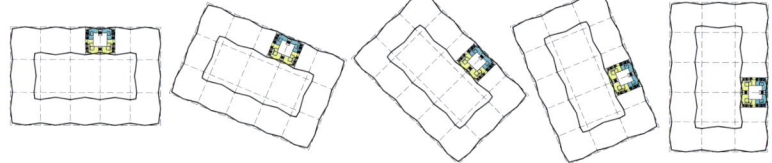

The regular entries, balconies, and shadows break up this linear facade.

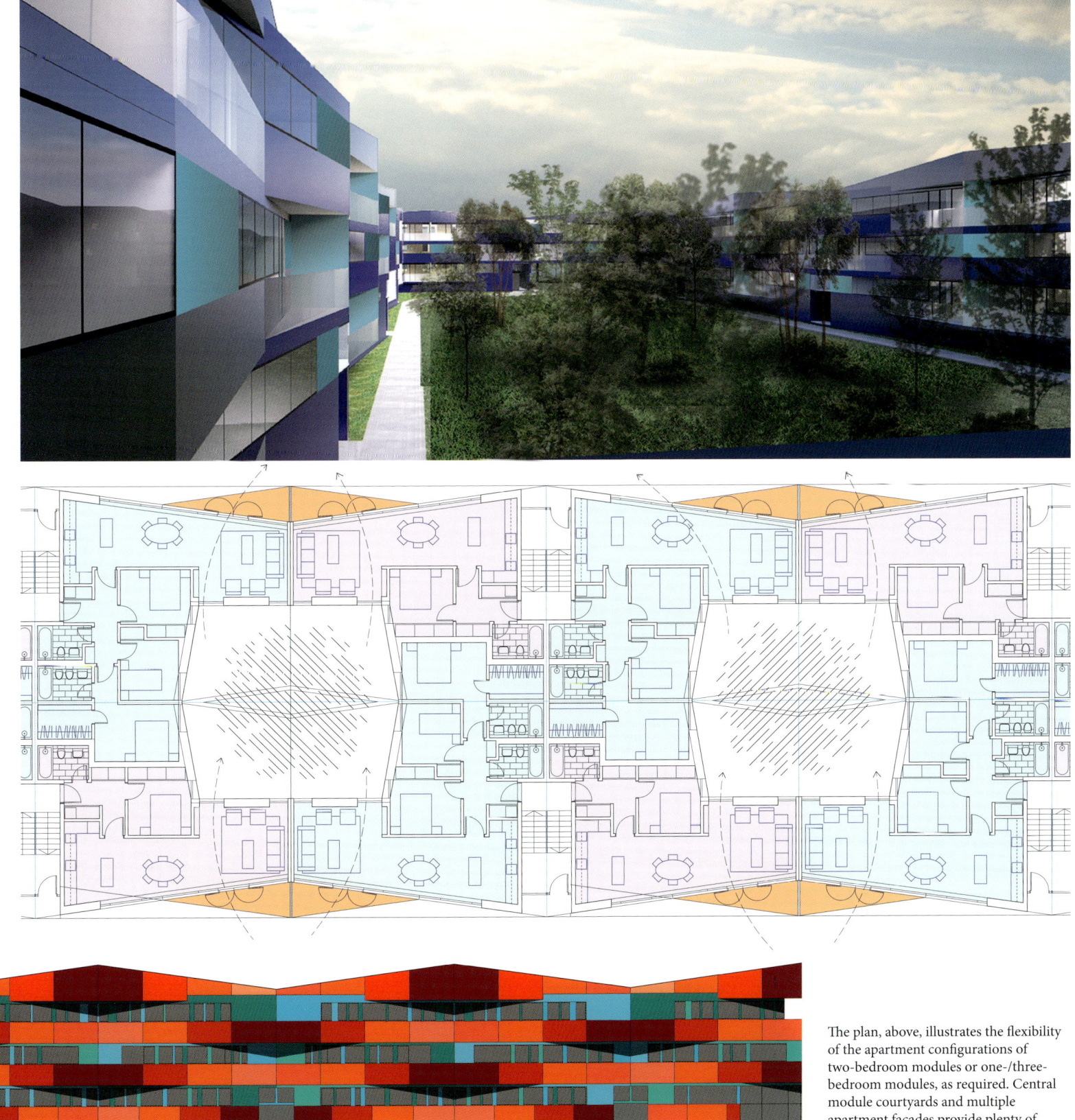

The plan, above, illustrates the flexibility of the apartment configurations of two-bedroom modules or one-/three-bedroom modules, as required. Central module courtyards and multiple apartment facades provide plenty of cross-ventilation and sun exposure.

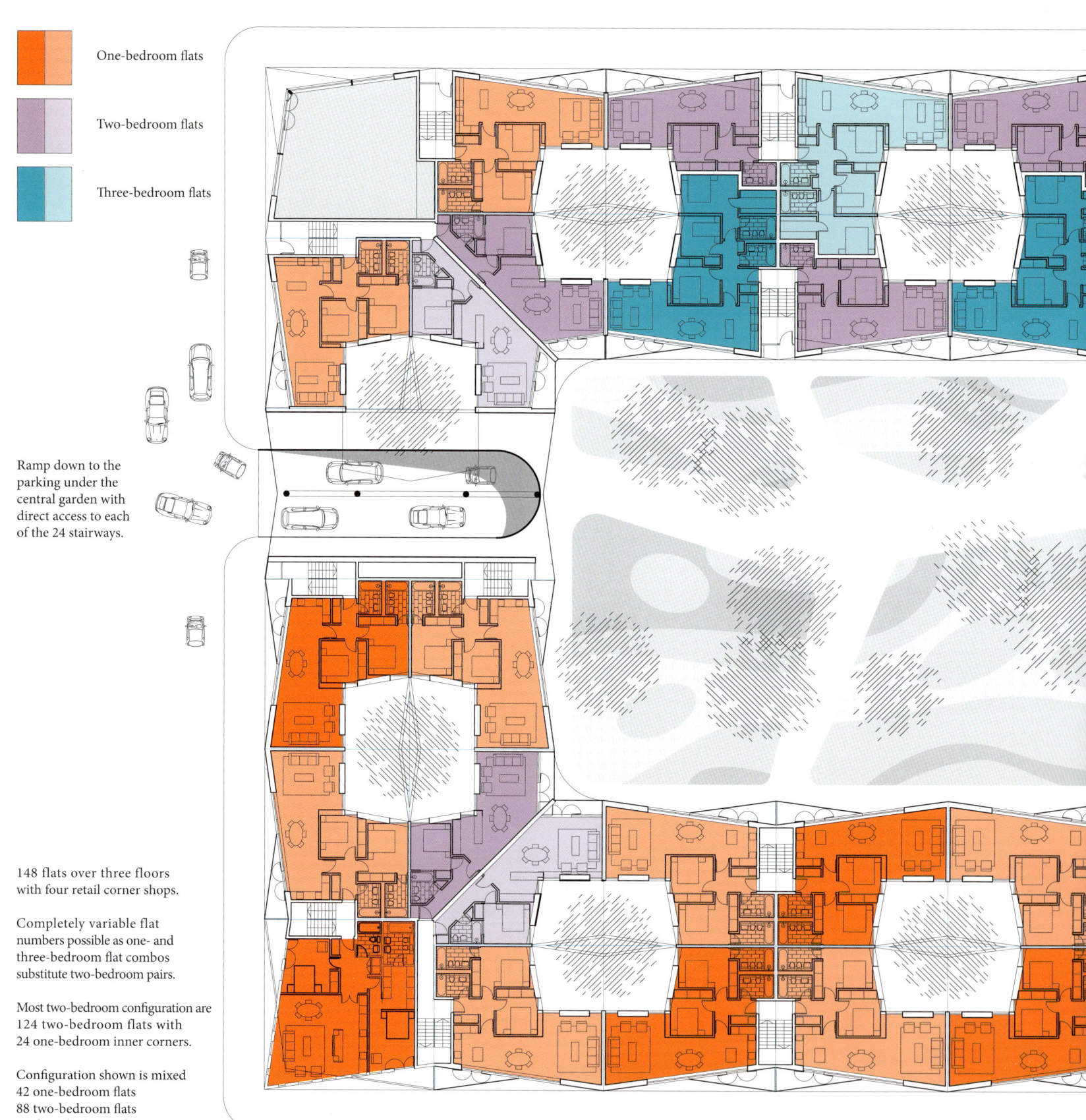

One-bedroom flats

Two-bedroom flats

Three-bedroom flats

Ramp down to the
parking under the
central garden with
direct access to each
of the 24 stairways.

148 flats over three floors
with four retail corner shops.

Completely variable flat
numbers possible as one- and
three-bedroom flat combos
substitute two-bedroom pairs.

Most two-bedroom configuration are
124 two-bedroom flats with
24 one-bedroom inner corners.

Configuration shown is mixed
42 one-bedroom flats
88 two-bedroom flats
18 three-bedroom flats.

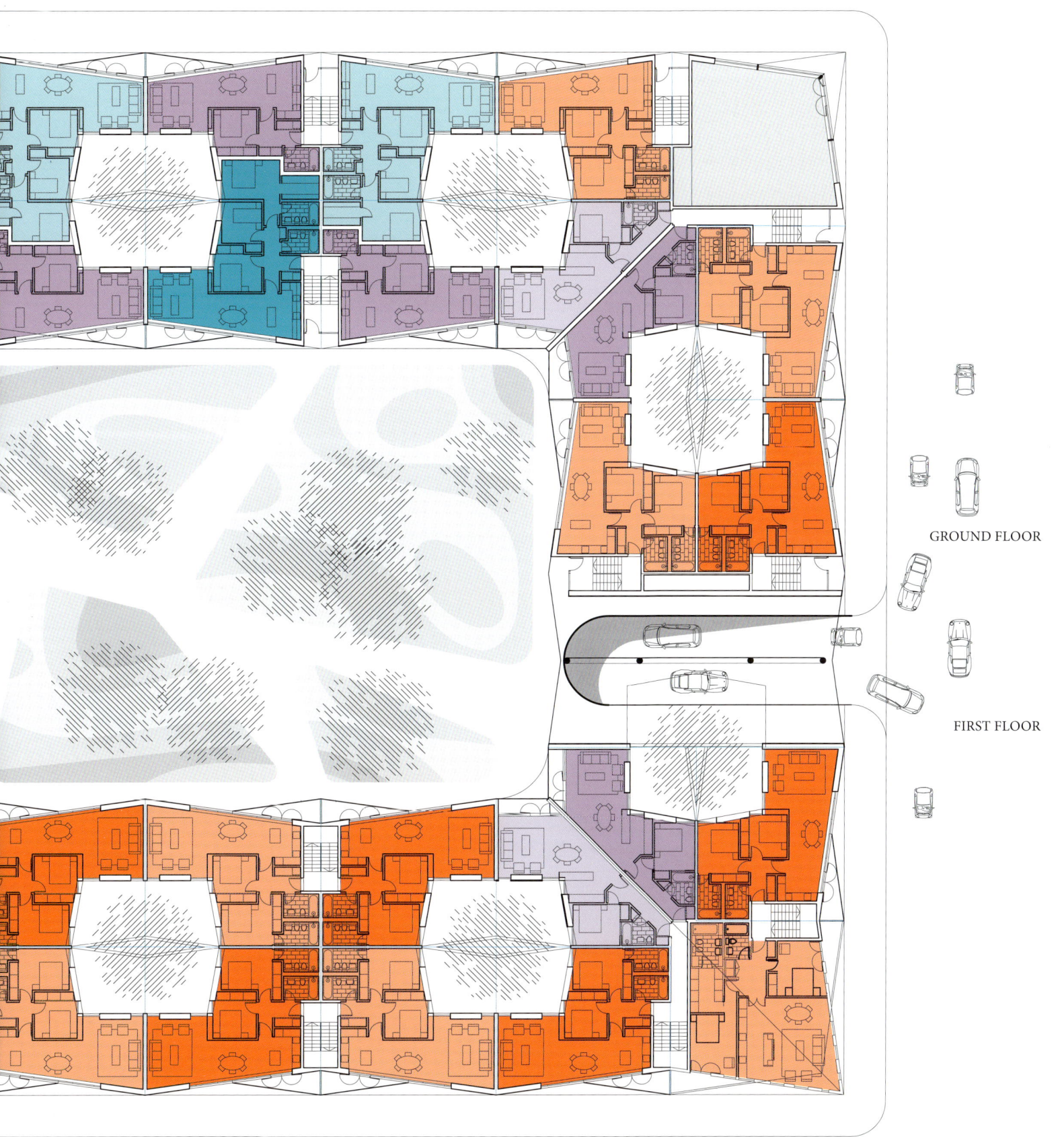

GROUND FLOOR

FIRST FLOOR

Procter-Rihl, London, UK
Topo Shelves
limited edition shelving, 1996-1998

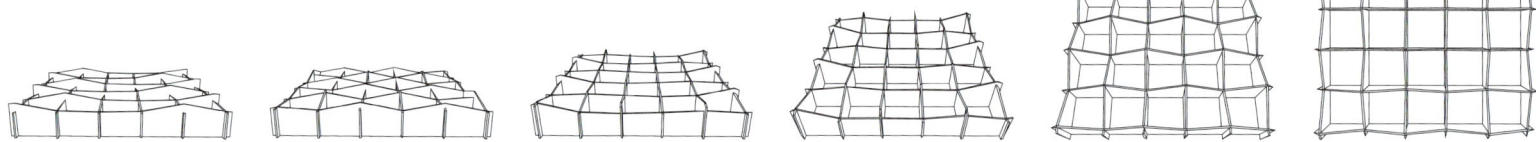

"Topo 7x7" (below) prototypes were selected for an exhibition auction called Futures by Bonhams in 1998. The Topo 7x7 with prismatic aesthetics was "woven" in 6 mm birch ply and 6 mm plastic. Two pieces were made as opposites, one with four pieces of birch ply the other with only four pieces of blue plastic.

Topo explores topographic contours using flat components. The flat pack shelving system of birch and translucent blue plastic components has shelves and uprights that slot together. The unit was designed to have a three-dimensional undulating front face defining a prismatic structure. Inspiration comes from geographic contours and shading devices found in modernist buildings in South America. The first two prototypes (left images) were developed in 1996 with extremly thin 6 mm materials and a smaller 7x7 bay module (200 mm square x 30 mm depth). In 1997 the limited production of 30 pieces were developed with 1 mm thick components and larger 5x5 module (182 mm square x 37 mm depth) sized for record albums or large books. Topo shelving was an early example of using Computer Numeric Control technology in 1996 to produce limited edition furniture in Europe.

Topo was tested in a series of configurations. Below, a one-off unit 2x5 counter developed for a DJ in 1 mm plastic and birch plywood.

Flow Shelves

limited edition shelving, 1998–1999

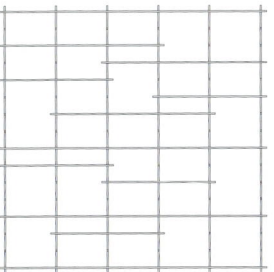

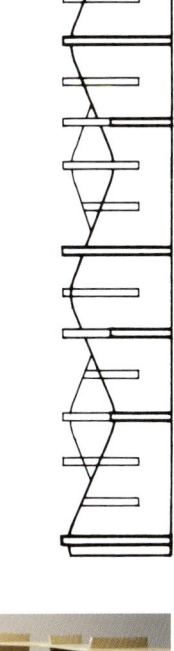

Flow follows similar principles as the Topo shelving, although with rounded flowing lines and multiple adjustable shelf slots. It was first shown at 100% Design in 1998 (drawing above) as a 227 mm square, but unlike the Topo it can be an infinitely extendable system. Any number of uprights can be configured with different length shelves linking across them to weave it to required width. It was designed to be randomly assembled by the user following the basic principle of the reversed rythym of peaks and valleys. The system led to some special commissions such as a nine metre long letterbox structure for an apartment lobby and a continuous library system. Flow was developed in two shades of dyed natural and dark brown 12 mm. All pieces slot together with the only fixing of wired rear bracing.

The system led to some special commissions such as the continuous library system shown above.

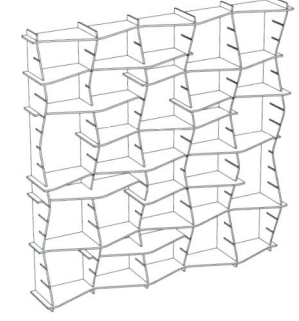

Flow allows a variety of shelf heights unlike a grid system.

Tok&Stok, Brazil
Topo Modular Unit—TMU
production shelving, 2008 to present
Pure Design Canada, 2000-2004

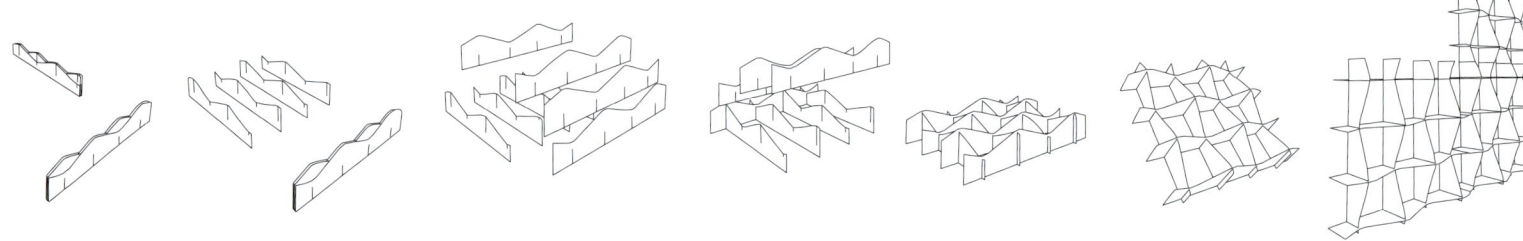

Single unit TMU in coated MDF for Tok&Stok, Brazil 2008–current.

Production in birch plywood, Pure Design, Canada. 2000–2004, four module stacked shelving system (below).

TMU is a continuing development on the Topo storage system exploring shipping, handling and assembly as key criteria for larger manufacturing production. The original topo piece had a prismatic aesthetic while a softer rounded aesthetic was developed for production. It was also made as a smaller three and a half module grid that when stacked or extended became a seven module unit. The production employs the CNC process with low cost material. First developed with Pure Design, Canada, in birch ply as a range of shelving and small CD units from 2000–2004 and sold widely across North America. The piece is now being produced by Tok&Stok in Brazil with a further development of the fixing systems and change of material. The use of melamine coated MDF in black and white brought another element to the design of a sharper graphic quality. Instead of covering the edge with a melamine strip, the studio decided to leave the MDF exposed to accentuate its flowing lines. New concave and convex corner components were developed in 2000 to allow more flexibility. The addition of the corners allowed the system to flow around corners or zigzag.

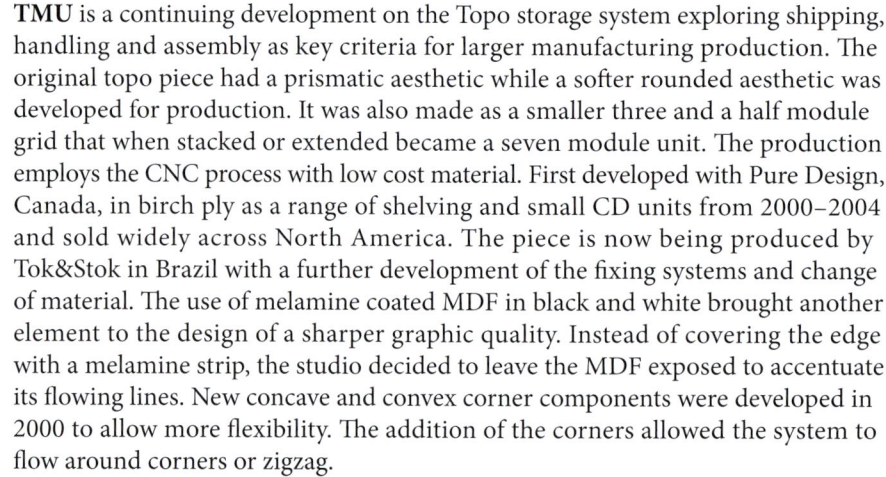

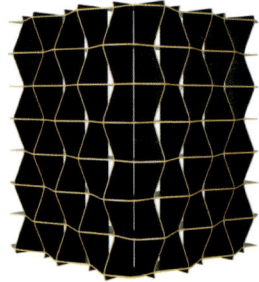

Convex and concave corners were developed (above) for the Tok&Stok line in Brazil. Units developed in two colours: black and white (below).

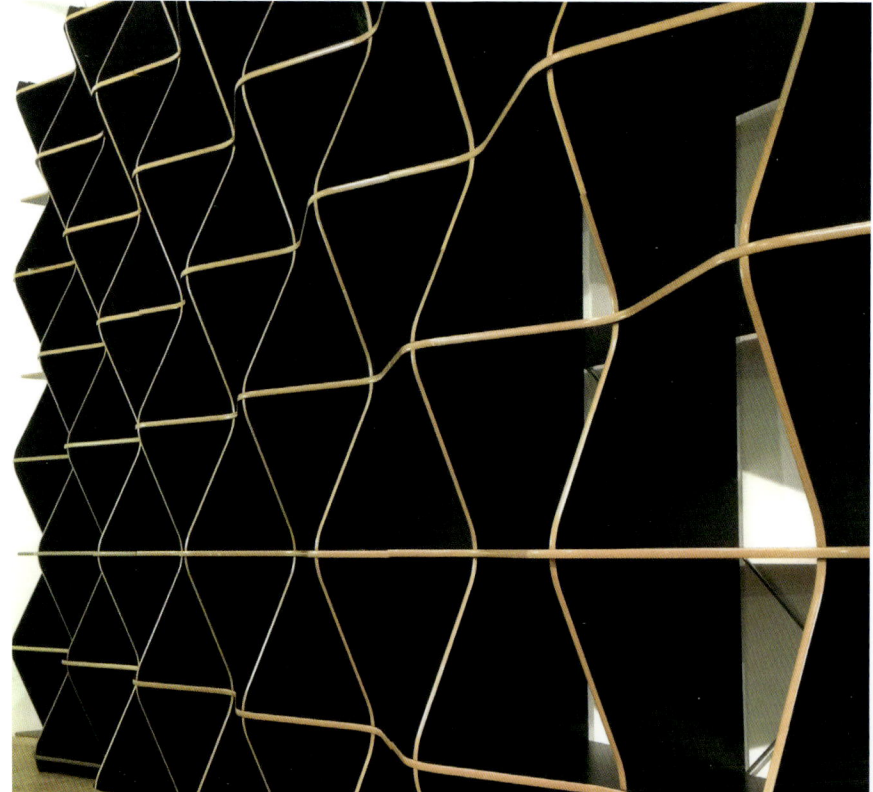

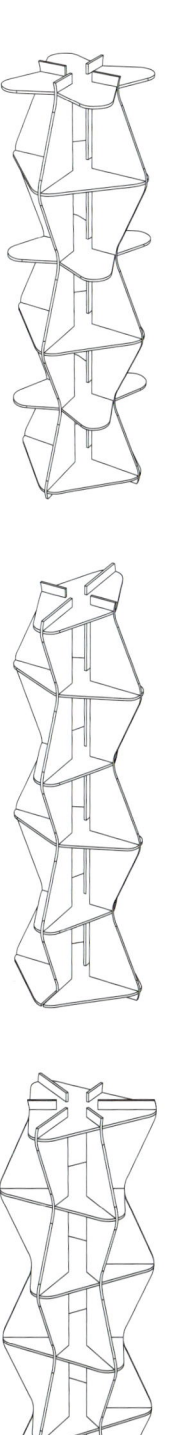

The tower is a new typology for storage and display units. They were originally developed as one-off pieces for an exhibition in 1997. Clover, Diamond and a Triangle patterns were developed for Cocada Preta, Brazil.

Procter-Rihl, London, UK
Nest Sofa
one-off sofa, Salone Satelite, Milan, 2000

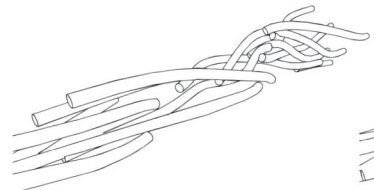 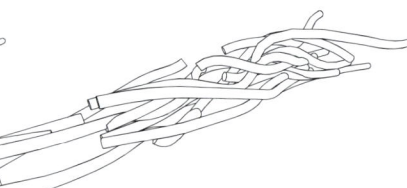 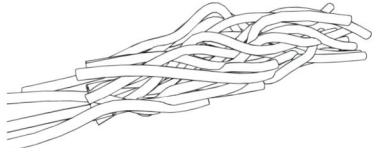 

Nest explores the concept of woven strands gathered to form a soft mass for seating. This frameless sofa made of skimmed coated polyurethane or stuffed tubes is woven randomly together as a nest and given shape by strategic straps. The design allows many arrangements and configurations as single or multiple seating. It works well as a larger set of pieces as shown (left) in the study models. Multiple colour strands create a sense of play and variety. The prototype made from dyed fire hoses was first shown at Milan Satellite show in 2000. *Abitare* magazine referred to it as a tri-dimmensional carpet, a new seating typology.

Salone Satellite with Kaleidoscope screens behind, Milan, April 2000. (far right). Clay studies (top and right). Simulation (below).

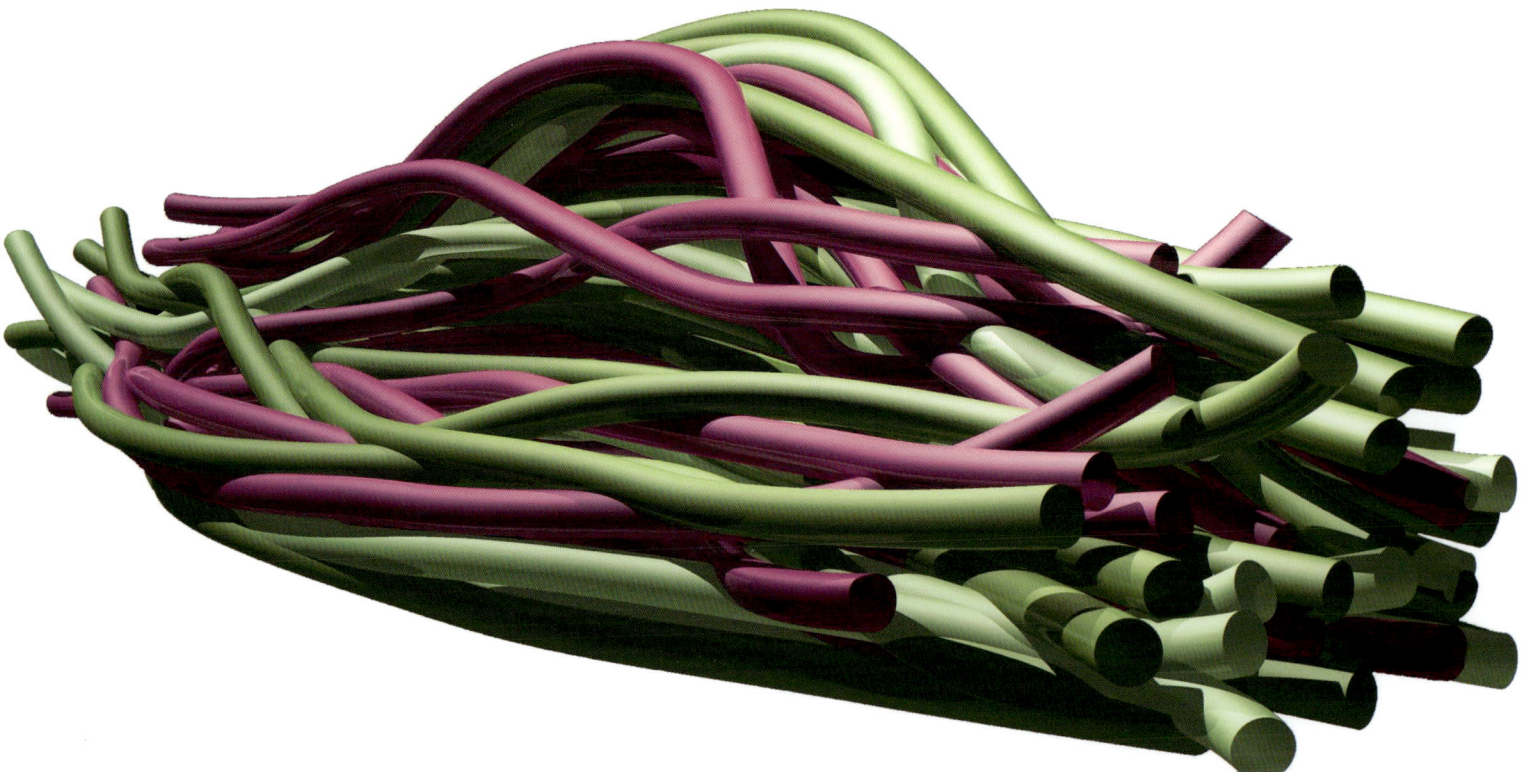

Selected Magazines

Summa, Argentina, Arquetipos e Abstracoes (Pull House)   Oct 2012
BD-Building Design, Vermont Radicals, London UK, (Pull)   10 Sept 2010
Arquine, Mexico, (Slice House)   Oct 2007
Pasajes Arquitectura y Critica, America Iberica, iss 89, Spain, (Slice)   Sept 2007
Lotus, issue 130, Italy, (Slice House)   Sept 2007
Observer, UK, (Corinne Road Flat)   2007
Decorate, Spain, (Slice House) Oct 2006
Barzon, Argentina, (Slice House)   Sept 2006
Vimagazino, Greece, (Slice House)   July 2006
Detail Publication IW, Taiwan, (Slice House)   July 2006
Enlace, Mexico, (Slice House)   July 2006
Independent Sat, London UK, (Slice House)   1 July 2006
Summa Arch and Design, Argentina, (Slice House)   June 2006
IW, Taiwan, (Slice House)   June 2006
World of Interiors, UK, (Slice House)   May 2006
Ambient, Slovenia, (Slice House, cover feature)   April 2006
Arquitetura & Construcao, Portugal, (Slice House)   May 2006
Max Magazine, Germany, (Brazilian culture article / Slice House)   Mar 2006
Attitude, issue 07, Portugal, (Slice House)   Jan 2006
SA Magazine, Singapore, (RIBA awards/ Slice House)   Dec 2005
Arq, Chile, (Slice House)   Dec 2005
AV, issue 102, Madrid, Spain, (Slice House)   Dec 2005
Ehlite, Switzerland, (Luxury Article/ Slice House)   Dec 2005
Icon, UK, (Slice House)   Nov 2005
Mark magazine - another architecture, Netherlands, (Slice House)   Oct 2005
AU, Brazil, (Slice House, cover feature)   Oct 2005
Ottagono, Milan, Italy, (Slice House)   Sept 2005
Highrise, Canada, (Slice House)   Fall 2005
Casa Vogue, Brazil, (Slice House)   Sept 2005
Neutra, Seville, Spain, (Slice House)   Aug 2005
Monument Architecture Design, Australia, (Slice House)   Aug 2005
AU, 20 year anniversy issue, Brazil, (Slice House)   July 2005
RIBA Journal, UK, (RIBA awards review Slice House)   July 2005
Arq/A, Portugal, (Slice House)   July /Aug 2005
L'Architecture d'Ajourd'hui, France, (Slice House)   July/ Aug 2005
BD, issue 1696, UK, (Architect of the Year Shortlisted/Slice)   28 Oct 2005
BD-Building Design Magazine, UK, (works feature Slice House)   July 2005
Architectural Journal, UK, (Slice/ RIBA awards, no. 23)   16 June 05
30-60, Magazine vol.3 Complex Geometry, Argentina, (Slice)   Sept 2004
Daily Telegraph Newspaper, UK, (procter:rihl profile-arch week)   23 June 2001
Architectural Review, UK, (Chelsea Flower Show)   July 2000
Wallpaper, UK, (architectural issue, Procter:Rihl)   July 2000
Blueprint, UK, (Chelsea Flower Show)   June 2000
Wallpaper, UK, (Chelsea Flower Show)   June 2000
BD-Building Design Magazine, UK, (Chelsea Flower Show)   June 2000
Abitare, issue 371, Italy, (Soho Penthouse)   March 1998
Abitare, issue 369, Italy, (Ozone table, Space Lilies)   Jan 1998
Architects' Journal, UK, (Soho Penthouse)   27 Nov 1997
Experimenta 18, Do it Yourself: Diseno Britanico, Spain, (profile) Nov 1997
Blueprint, issue 144, UK, (Blueprint Exhibition Stand)   Nov 1997
New York Times Newspaper, USA,(Ozone table, Space Lily) 30 Oct 1997
Architects' Journal, UK, (Topo shelves)   Oct 1997
Blueprint 142, Blueprint Awards sel. by Verner Panton, UK, (Topo)   Sept 1997
Guardian Weekend, UK, (Breaking the Mould -Prion boxes)   18 Jan 1997
Wallpaper issue 2, UK, (Profile, Strata tables, Prion boxes)   Jan 1997
Evening Standard Newspaper, UK, (The Young Lions-profile)   2 Oct 1996
Blueprint issue 132, UK, (Topo shelving)   Oct 1996
The Times Newspaper, UK (Ozone table)   21 Sept 1996

Selected Books

2016
Renovations, RIBA publications, London, UK (Scoop). pp 172–175, June 2016
2013
Introduction to Modern Architecture, Compositore, Bologna. (Slice).
Total Sing. Housing, Important Houses of the 1st decade 21 Cent, Actar (Slice)
Architectural Guide Brazil, L.Kimmel, DOM Pub, BR (Slice) p 276
2012
The Best of Grand Designs, Kevin McCloud, HarperCollins, UK (Slice House)
2011
Razao Ambiente, L Calvalcanti, Museu de Arte Moderna, Sao Paulo, BR (Slice)
2010
Atlas Arch. of the 21st Cent, Fernandez-Galiano, F. BBVA, Spain (Slice House)
Affordable Houses: Houses on a Budget, S Crafti, Images Publ., Aus. (Slice)
2009
100 Country Houses: New Rural Arch., Beth Brown, Images Publ., Aus. (Pull)
2008
Phaidon Atlas 21st Century World Architecture, Phaidon Press (Pull and Slice)
Strike a Pose, Eccentric Arch. and Spectacular Spaces, Germany (Pull and Slice)
2G Dossier Emerging Ibero-Amer Architecture, Ed. Gustavo Gili, Spain (Slice)
Lux. Houses Top of the World, M. Kunz & M.Roth, teNeues,Germany (Slice)
Architettura Cont. Brasile, R.Anelli, Motta Archittettura, Italy (Slice)
Pool Design, Daab, Germany, (Slice House)
2007
1001 Buildings to See Before You Die, Octopus, UK (Pull and Slice Houses)
2006
Case Latino Americane, Electa, Italy (Slice House)
Casas Brasileiras, Mosley & Viana, Brazil (Slice House)
Contemporary Architecture in Latin America, Thames & Hudson, UK (Slice)
Houses International Atlas, Casey Mathewson, Feierabend, (Slice, P:R profile)
Quadro da Arquitetura Brasileira Exh. Catalogue, Italy, Spain (Slice House)
Architectural Inspirations, Daab, Germany, (Slice House)
Encore Moderne? Arch. Contemporaine au Brésil Exh., Paris, FR (Slice House)
Tropical Minimal, Danielle Miller, Thames&Hudson, UK, (Slice House)
2005
150 Best House Ideas Book, HDI Publ./Loft Publ., Spain (Slice House)
The New House, Links Publications, Barcelona, Spain (Slice House) pp 130–139
Algarve Housing Competition catalogue, Silves, Portugal (Tile House)
XXXSmall Houses, by Casey Mathewson, Feierabend, Berlin, (Slice House)
2004
IV Latin American Architecture Biennale catalogue Lima, Peru (Slice House)
Jovens Arquitetos Brasileiros, R. Segre, Mosley & Vianna, BR, (Slice House)
Internt'l Design Yearbook 2004, Ed. Tom Dixon, Laurence King, UK (Super8)
2003
Design UK2, ConranPubl., London, UK, (Profile/ Yoga CD rack)
2001
New Architects II, Ed. Arch Foundation, Merrel Publ., UK (3Elipses/ Chelsea)
Internt'l Design Yearbook 2001, Ed.M. deLucchi, Laurence King, UK (Flow)
Review of Design Icons, Arts Book International, UK (Procter:Rihl Profile)
1999
MNM, Minimalist Interiors, Loft Publications, Spain (BentoBox penthouse)
1998
50 Products: Innov. in Design & Mat'ls, Mel Byars, RotoVision, CH (SpaceLily)
New Designers Book, New British Designers, UK (Procter Rihl)
Internt'l Design Yearbook 1998, Ed.Richard Sapper, Laurence King,UK (Topo)
New Architects: Britain's best young practices, Booth-Clibborn,UK (BentoBox)

Awards

MCHAP Emerging Architecture, USA, (Slice house), Nominated- April 2014
Grand Design Awards - Int'l House, UK, (Pull House), Finalist- May 2010
Museu da Casa Brasileira, Sao Paulo, Brazil, (TMU), 2nd Prize- Nov 2008
Grand Design Awards - Single Dwelling, UK, (Slice), Finalist- May 2006
Architect of the Year - Single Dwelling, UK, (Slice House), Finalist- Nov 2005
Concrete Centre Sustainability Award, UK, (Slice House), Finalist- Nov 2005
RIBA Award , first Award in South America, (Slice House), Award- Jun 2005
IV Latin Amer. Arch. Biennale, Peru, (Slice House), Finalist Brazil- Oct 2004
RHS Chelsea Flower Show, London, (Show Garden), Gold Medal- May 2000

Architecture Exhibitions

10+10 exh/ Brazilian Architecture, AzW Gallery, Vienna, Austria, Nov 2013
Living Spaces City, Found. Clovis Salgado, Belo Horizonte, Brazil, Feb 2012
Living Spaces City, Institute Tomie Ohtake, Sao Paulo, Brazil, April 2011
Ecological Reason Ambiance, Mus. of Mod. Art, Sao Paulo, Brazil, April 2011
Panorama Brazilian Architecture, Columbia Univ., NYC, USA, July 2010
Regents Place, Building Centre, London, UK, (ReVerse it Plaza) Summer 2007
Quadro da Arquitetura Brasileira, Italy & Spain, (Slice House) March 2006
Encore Moderne, Inst. Francais Arch., Paris, (Slice House) Oct 2005–Jan 2006
Sao Paulo Arch. Biennale, Sao Paulo, Brazil, (Slice House) October 2005
Summer Nights, Arch. Found., The Yard, London, UK, (Houses) Aug 2005
Algarve Housing, Granturismo, Silves, Portugal, (Tile House) Aug 2005
IV Latin American Architecture Biennale, Lima, Peru, (Slice) Sept 2004
Open Practice Architecture Week, London, UK, (Current Projects) June 2004
RHS Chelsea Flower Show, London, UK, (Gold Medal Garden), May 2000
New Architects, best young practices in Britain, Glasgow, Scotland, Jan 1999
Contemporary Gems, Arch'l Dialogues, London, UK, (Penthouse) Mar 1996

Selected Design Exhibitions

Premio Design MCB, Casa da Brasiliera, Sao Paulo, Brazil, (TMU) Nov 2008
Design UK 2, Viaduct Gallery, London, UK, (Yoga CD rack) Sept 2003
Clear Cut, Research CNC Plastic Tech, London, UK, (Super8/tables) Sept 2002
procter:rihl @ Christophe Lemaire, Paris and Tokyo, (Kaleidoscope) May 2000
procter:rihl, Salone Satellite, Milan, Italy, (Nest, Kaleidoscope) April 2000
Design Britannique, Chateau de Bosmelet, Auffay, France, (Flow) May 1999
procter:rihl, DUB exhibition, Salone Milan, Italy (Topo, Strata) April 1999
procter:rihl @ Colette, Paris (99, Prion, Space Lily, Strata) Jan 1999
Biennale International Design 98, Saint Etienne, France, (Space Lily) Nov 1998
Fish + Chips, British Design, stilwerk gallery, Hamburg, Germany, Oct 1998
procter:rihl, 100% Design, London, UK, (Web, Flow) Sept 1998
Objects of our Time, Amer. Craft Mus., NYC, (Prion, SpaceLily) May 1998
DesignUK, Totem Gallery, NYC, USA, (Topo Tower, Space Lily) April 1998
Plastics, Black Swan Guild, Frome Somerset, UK, (Prion, Space Lily) Apr 1998
Salon du Meuble, by Yoichi Nakamuta, Paris, France, (Topo Tower) Jan 1998
UK Now, British Design sponser Dti, Melb., Aus, (Prion, Space Lily) Nov 1997
Int'l Furniture Fair Tokyo, Japan, (Topo, Strata, Prion, Space Lily) Nov 1997
Objects of our Time, Crafts Council; London, Belfast, Edinburgh, 1996/97
procter:rihl, 100% Design, London, UK, (Space Lily, Glacial,Topo) Sept 1997
New British Design, Galerie Andrea Leenarts, Cologne (Prion) Jan 1997
procter:rihl, 100% Design, Kings Road, London, UK, (Strata, Ozone) Sept 1996
New British Designers, Tombolini, Milan, Italy, (Ozone table) July1996
Int'l Contemporary Furniture Fair, NYC, USA (Topo, Strata, Prion) May 1996
Products of Desire 2, by architects, RIBA, London, UK, (Ozone) April 1996
procter:rihl, 100% Design, Kings Road, London, UK, (Prion,Ozone) Sept 1995

Photographers Credits

Helene Binet: p 88, p 89. Bernard Hoffman: p 6 middle. Trillium1000: p 6 bottom. Robert Damora: p 11. Leonardo Finotti: p 8 middle and bottom, p 11 top middle, p 12 top and top middle, p 47 bottom, p 48 bottom, p 50, p 53 left, p 54 left, p 73. Nelson Kon: p 9 top, p 11 middle bottom and bottom. Sue Barr: p 5 bottom, p 11 middle, p 44 middle and right, p 45, p 48 top, middle, and main, p 51 main and top, p 52, p 54 middle and right, p 80, p 81, p 82, p 83. Bandits: p 5 top, p 16 bottom, p 40, p 41, p 44 top, p 46, p 47, p 51 bottom, p 54 top, p 85. Reserva Ibiopoca, MG Brazil: p 8 middle Joaquim Bergamin p 31, p 63, p 69 left and middle, p 88, p 89, p 106, p 107. Other photographs by Chris Procter, Fernando Rihl.

Artifice books on architecture   t: +44 (0)20 7713 5097
10a Acton Street, London, WC1X 9NG   e: sales@artificebooksonline.com
United Kingdom   www.artificebooksonline.com

Book Editing and Design
Christopher Procter and Fernando Rihl

All opinions expressed within this publication are those of the authors and not necessarily of the publisher.

British Library in Cataloguing Data. A CIP record for this book is available from the British Library

ISBN 978 908967 40 4

Every effort has been made to trace the copyright holders, but if any have been inadvertently overlooked the necessary arrangements will be made at the first opportunity.

Artifice books on architecture, London, UK, is an environmentally responsible company. *Architecture and Beyond: Procter-Rihl* is printed on sustainably sourced paper.

Artifice
books on architecture